666

AND ALL THAT
THE TRUTH ABOUT THE FUTURE

JOHN DICKSON AND GREG CLARKE

AQUILA
PRESS

PO Box A 287, Sydney South 1235, Australia
Ph: (612) 8268 3344
Fax: (612) 2868 3357
Email: sales@youthworks.net
Web: www.youthworks.publications.net

666 and all that – The truth about the future
Published July 2007
Copyright Aquila Press 2007 © John Dickson and Greg Clarke

National Library of Australia
ISBN 978 1921137 808

Cover design by Rachel Heriot
Typeset by Lankshear Design

John's dedication

FOR MARIE

A Toi la gloire, O Ressuscité
A Toi la victoire Pour l'éternité!

Greg's dedication

FOR THE FEY

Contents

Introduction   7

1. The three dimensions of the Christian life   11

2. How to 'read' the future   25

3. The Rapture, Israel, and other Christian myths   37

4. The personal apocalypse: a Christian
   understanding of death   51

5. Ready or not: the future arrival of Jesus   65

6. Beyond 'fire-and-brimstone'   81

7. The future of evil   95

8. The three targets of God's judgment   107

9. The fate of those who have never heard the gospel   119

10. Life *after* life-after-death   135

11. The end of the world as we know it—or is it?   151

12. The future Genesis   161

13. Why heaven is not enough   169

14. The Bible's last word   181

Endnotes   195

Introduction

Confessions of an apocalyptic youth

JOHN. In my first decade as a Christian, as a 15 to 25-year-old, I was absolutely mesmerised by the 'apocalyptic' aspects of the Bible. The Second Coming, Hell, the Beast, 666 and all that: these themes fascinated me. I daydreamed about them, prayed about them, told others about them. I even wrote songs about them. Unfortunately, incriminating evidence of my apocalyptic youth is a matter of public record.

The first album my band recorded back in 1988 (an 'LP' at that) was ominously titled *Things to Come*. The front cover featured the band looking longingly over Sydney's Palm Beach toward a distant sunrise—a not-so-subtle image of our future hope. The theme wove its way through the entire album. Track 2, side one (music discs used to have two sides) is a song called 'Waiting Here':

Yes I'm waiting here,
Watching moments, As they disappear into the years,
I read the things you've said,
I watch my world, And I look ahead,
Cos I see the things you've said.
Yes I'm waiting here, Waiting for you to appear,
and it can't be long; it can't be long.

I look back on all this and, frankly, I am a little embarrassed not just about the 80s haircuts and 3-chord song-writing but mainly about my heart-on-sleeve apocalyptic zeal as a 20-year-old Christian singer.

If I am honest, such longing for the future seems a little foreign to me now. It is not prominent in my daily thoughts; it hasn't featured much in my preaching in recent years; and I have not written a song on the topic for well over a decade. 'Eschatology'—from the Greek word *eschatos* or *last things* —was once front-and-centre in my life. Now it is neatly packed away somewhere in my brain's theological sub-directory.

I'll explain later *why* I think this is. Right now I simply want to admit that, despite the silly speculations and potential extremes associated with an apocalyptic outlook, I suspect my youthful longing for Christ's return and for God's eternal kingdom was not too far from the biblical viewpoint after all. Whacky stuff aside, what the Bible *really* says about the future has begun to take hold of me again capturing my imagination and intellect and causing me to rethink (and re-engage with) the here-and-now.

Anxious for answers

GREG. My path has been a little different from John's. I didn't really have the same apocalyptic youthful zeal. I grew up in a strong Christian home, but one in which 'the last things' weren't an obsession. But in late high school, music and literature alerted me to the anxieties and puzzles of death. Listening to bands like *The Cure* and *The Smiths*, with their gothic and pessimistic takes on human existence, and reading confronting literature such as

Samuel Beckett's bleak play, *Waiting For Godot*, I found myself trying to sort out the various views on offer of the afterlife, judgment and the end of the world. (Don't worry—I also played plenty of cricket and wore colours other than black.)

Having now written two theses on the subject, I feel I've made a lot of progress in understanding what is going to happen in the future—as well as what *isn't going to happen.* Through really reading the Bible, rather than relying on second-hand reports of what it teaches, I've come to a fairly settled view on the Now, the Not-Yet, and the Not-Likely!

My motivation hasn't been just to sort out my own thoughts. Obsession with eschatology has divided Christian churches and occupied endless hours for many Christians. The incredible publishing success of the *Left Behind*[1] series of novels and films—works which John and I consider to be less than helpful and true—has left me itching to offer an alternative view, something with hopefully a finer ear for the biblical literature on the subject; something that isn't trapped within Western triumphalistic culture and the politics of Armageddon; something with less heat and more light.

By blending an exploration of the biblical material with discussion of eschatology in Christian and secular culture, we hope to have provided a reality check on this hot and controversial topic. We also hope that we have served to make 'eschatology' simpler than the word suggests and a lot simpler than its strange flowcharts of dispensations and pictures of many-headed beasts often suggest. What we know of the future of the world is not as complex as many people think. And yet acting on that knowledge is often far removed from a Christian's daily life. At least, that has been our experience.

And so this book poses as much of a challenge to us, as authors, as it does to our fellow believers—will our knowledge of God's future shape our lives? As we look together at what the Bible says (and does not say) about the future, we expect many readers will be disturbed, comforted, humbled and (hopefully) thrilled. We expect that some cherished beliefs may get rattled, some confirmed, and others be discovered anew. We trust that your understanding of what is knowable about God's future will be clarified, refined and expanded.

If you are not a follower of Christ, but have picked up this book out of interest in the Christian view of the future, we hope your world will have changed at least a bit by the time you finish reading. Our journey towards understanding what God has promised about the future has been a long one, and is still in motion. Our prayer is that you will undertake the journey with us, that we might end up together with the coming Lord.

John Dickson & Greg Clarke

1 | The three dimensions of the Christian life

I F WE HAD TO SUM UP what it's like to be a Christian here and now, we couldn't do better than the Apostle Paul's words to the Corinthians (often heard at weddings, for good reason):

> 1 CORINTHIANS 13:13. And now these three remain: faith, hope and love. But the greatest of these is love.

The reference to 'love', of course, recalls the central ethical command of Jesus to 'love your neighbour as yourself'. 'Faith' here refers to our trust in God's mercy guaranteed by Jesus' death and resurrection. The Christian life, then, is lived through *faith* in Jesus, *love* for God and others, and *hope* … but for what?

It is crucial to observe that Paul places 'hope'—our eager expectation of God's promised future—right alongside 'faith' and 'love' (albeit with 'love' getting the gold medal). This is the triumvirate of the Christian life, the three things governing the shape of the true believer. If we lack any of these, we are in danger of becoming a distorted image of a follower of Christ.

Hope can sometimes be the 'poor cousin' of love and faith for Christians, barely considered and rarely explored. We need to rectify that, firstly by exploring what hope is all about.

Christian 'hope' is not wishful thinking. Nor is it the pie-in-the-sky longing some people feel about winning the lottery (or Greg and John feel about joining U2). It is more like the anticipation you might feel as the time approaches for your pre-booked First Class round-the-world holiday. Throughout the Bible, hope is our *eager expectation of God's promised future*. It's the yearning, desiring, pressing forward part of Christian life—the part that makes everything here and now seem worthwhile.

Hope of this kind is at the *core* of biblical faith. In fact, the simple point we want to make in this first chapter is that Christianity has *three dimensions* and that without the third dimension of hope, our Christian lives will be flat and unbalanced, a mere shadow of the biblical reality.

We should be clear: these three words were not just plucked out of the air by Paul in a moment of poetic flair. Nor did he pull them together for the particular benefit of the Corinthians alone. Faith, hope and love appear everywhere in Paul's writings. For example, a few years earlier, the Apostle wrote to his beloved Thessalonians:

> 1 THESSALONIANS 1:2–3. We continually remember before our God and Father your work produced by *faith*, your labour prompted by *love*, and your endurance inspired by *hope* in our Lord Jesus Christ.[2]

A decade later Paul would open his letter to the church at Colossae in this way:

> COLOSSIANS 1:4–5. We have heard of your *faith* in Christ Jesus and of the *love* you have for all the saints—the *faith* and *love* that spring from the *hope* that is stored up for you in heaven.

Nor is this just a Paul thing. The Apostle Peter concludes one of his great hope passages with the same three dimensions of the Christian life:

> 1 PETER 1:21–22. Through him (Christ) you believe in God, who raised him from the dead and glorified him, and so

your *faith* and *hope* are in God. Now that you have purified yourselves by obeying the truth so that you have sincere *love* for your brothers, *love* one another deeply, from the heart.

Faith, hope and love are what you might call the *deep structure* of authentic Christianity. Pick up any chapter of the New Testament and it will almost certainly be about faith, love or hope, and sometimes it will be about all three together.[3]

The question that arises from all this is simple. Does *hope* have its rightful place in our Christian lives—right up there with faith and love? Most Christians are conscious of trying to build up their faith in God's incredible mercy in Jesus, and even the newest believer knows that living as a Christian essentially involves trying to love other people as God has loved us.

But what about hope? What part is played by this dimension of the Christian life in our thoughts, words and actions? Would others describe you not only as a person of faith and love, but as a person of hope, someone who eagerly awaits the future God has promised in his Word?

The four great hopes

So, what exactly do we hope for as Christians? What is the future we are meant to be so eagerly expecting? We think it boils down to four things, each of which we will tackle in detail in the rest of the book. For now, we want to offer an overview of these great hopes so that you can have a clear idea of the shape of God's promised future.

Firstly, it is fairly obvious that one of the fundamental things Christians eagerly expect is the so-called 'second coming' of Christ. Actually, the language of a 'second' coming is a little misleading because, from the perspective of the New Testament, the return of Christ at the climax of history is his *ultimate* coming. What occurred between 5BC—AD30[4] was not the full feature at all but a preview of the glorious arrival of the Messiah. The historical ministry of Jesus of Nazareth was, if you like, the advance notice of *who* is the coming Messiah, *what* he really stands for and *how* he is able to open up his kingdom even to guilty people like us. But it is only when Jesus arrives in universal glory that the Messiah's mission foretold in the Old Testament will be fully realised. (More about this in Chapter 5).

The second aspect of Christian hope has to do with the final judgment or, perhaps more accurately, final *justice*. A central role of the Messiah, according to both the Old and New Testaments, is to overthrow all that is opposed to the Creator. The first Christians longed for Judgment Day, not out of some macabre fascination with vengeance but because they longed for the wrongs of our world to be put to right. In this context, as weird as it sounds, 'Hell' (which will be explored in Chapter 6) becomes a cause of Christian praise.

Thirdly, the New Testament asks believers to look expectantly beyond the grave. We suspect there is a lot of confusion here in modern Christianity. Many suppose that the Bible's promise of 'eternal life' has to do with our 'souls' (whatever they are) resting evermore in God's heavenly presence (wherever that is). But where the New Testament does hint at such a thing—and it only *hints* at it—it makes perfectly clear that soul*ish* existence in a heavenly bliss is only at most a temporary arrangement until all the dead are resurrected for Judgment and those who belong to Jesus will enjoy a transformed *bodily* existence modelled on Christ's own resurrection. Eternal life in the Bible, then, is the *Resurrection Life* that follows what we often think of as life-after-death.[5]

This relates to the fourth and climactic aspect of Christian hope: God's new creation. The Bible—both Old and New Testaments—envisions the 'Kingdom Come' not as a soul*ish* eternity in a heavenly realm but as the reality of heaven come down to earth. The biblical promise of the resurrection of the body finds its counterpart in the pledge of a restored creation. We regard this as one of the most awe-inspiring, if sometimes neglected or misunderstood, teachings in the Bible.

This, in a nutshell, is the basic shape of biblical hope. These are the four things that constitute God's promised future. And, as we describe each of these in detail in the following pages, we will also be taking on some of the misconceptions and wild-goose-chases that have been associated with Christian thinking about the future. We'll be looking at what the Bible assures us is and is not going to happen.

But, first, we need to say something about the *basis* of our future hope.

The historical basis of our future hope

We have already said that in biblical usage 'hope' is not a pie-in-the-sky-when-you-die feeling; nor is it a wishful thinking born of the human longing for survival beyond the grave. Biblical hope is grounded in God's *previous* activity in the world. The events of the past are intimately connected with the promises about the future. To put it more precisely, our hope for Christ's return, the judgment of the world, the resurrection of the body and the renewal of creation is grounded in the prior activity of Jesus, in his teaching, miracles, death and rising to life. Jesus' earthly life was not only the 'preview' of his identity and character as the Messiah;

it was also the foretaste and guarantee of the Messiah's kingdom itself. We can see this in a number of ways.

Firstly, the miracles of Jesus—his healings, exorcisms and control over nature—were deliberate signs of the restoration of all things in God's future kingdom. Jesus states this explicitly in the words, "If I drive out demons by the Spirit of God, then the Kingdom of God has come upon you" (Matt 12:28). In other words, Jesus' divine powers were glimpses of the coming kingdom. In God's future kingdom, evil will be overthrown, frail bodies will be restored and nature itself will be renewed. Jesus pre-empted all of these things in his ministry of casting out evil spirits, healing the lame and blind and bringing order and blessing to the physical world itself (think of him calming a storm, multiplying food and turning water into wine). What will one day be fully realised in God's kingdom has been demonstrated in miniature in the deeds of Jesus. Our future hope is thus intimately connected with Christ's historical activity. The very fact that Jesus has shown us the Kingdom assures us that it exists, and is on its way.

Secondly, the raising of Jesus from the dead was another future reality brought into the present. Jesus' resurrection was not simply the proof of his status as Messiah; it was the demonstration of one of the Bible's fundamental promises about the future. The Old Testament insists that at the end of history God will raise the dead and revive creation (more about this when we discuss Isa 65:17–25 and Dan 12:1–4). This promise finds its divine guarantee—a down payment, you could say—within history in the resurrection of the Messiah. Jesus' rising to life is the first act of God's new creation or, as Paul puts it, the risen Jesus is the 'firstfruits' indicating that the full harvest is on the way (1 Cor 15:20–23).

Jesus' *death* was also a future event brought forward. What

Jesus endured on the cross on our behalf was the wrath due to us on the Day of Judgment (Rom 5:9). For those who have embraced the mercy secured by his death, the Judgment Day has, in a very real sense, already occurred. We have received advance notice of our divine acquittal because our sins were dealt with on a hill outside Jerusalem in AD 30. (We will say more about what the judgment will be like *for Christians* in Chapter 14.)

There is one last way in which our hopes about the future kingdom are grounded in God's past action. The gift of the Holy Spirit given to every believer is itself a down payment of a coming reality. This is a beautiful theme of Scripture but it requires a little explanation.

In the Old Testament God's future kingdom is described as a world fully possessed of God's Spirit. All of life will be revived and empowered by the breath or spirit—same word in Hebrew (*ruah*)—of the eternal God. So we read in the prophet Ezekiel:

> EZEKIEL 37:11–14. Then he said to me: "Son of man, these bones are the whole house of Israel. They say, 'Our bones are dried up and our hope is gone; we are cut off.' Therefore prophesy and say to them: 'This is what the Sovereign LORD says: O my people, I am going to open your graves and bring you up from them; I will bring you back to the land of Israel. Then you, my people, will know that I am the LORD, when I open your graves and bring you up from them. I will put my Spirit in you and you will live, and I will settle you in your own land. Then you will know that I the LORD have spoken, and I have done it, declares the LORD.'"[6]

The New Testament teaches that this future age of the Spirit is glimpsed in the gift of the Holy Spirit now. For instance, the Apostle Paul says that in advance of the Spirit-possessed life of the

Kingdom Come, God has given his children a 'deposit' on the future payment:

> EPHESIANS 1:13–14. Having believed, you were marked in him with a seal, the promised Holy Spirit, who is a deposit guaranteeing our inheritance until the redemption of those who are God's possession.

What is this 'inheritance' of which the Holy Spirit is a guarantee or deposit? It is the Spirit-filled life of God's future kingdom. There will come a day when God will breathe on his people (as Ezek 37 above promised) and they will come to new life in a new land. Until then, we have a down payment of that breath/Spirit which transforms our minds, enables us to serve one another and fits us out for the coming kingdom.[7] The gift of the Spirit now is a foretaste within history of the ultimate, Spirit-possessed life we will enjoy in God's coming kingdom.

History and future hope are intertwined. What God has done already guarantees what he has said he will do in the future. Hope, then, is not merely wishful thinking; it is a reasoned trust in what God has promised and foreshadowed in the ministry of Jesus and in the gift of the Holy Spirit.

More than a down payment?

One mistake Christians can make is to forget that hope is (of course) about the *future*. Some people, eager to claim the victory that Jesus has won over sin and death and suffering, expect *all* of God's good kingdom to come right here and now. The technical phrase for this is to have an 'over-realised eschatology', that is, to think that the future we long for is the reality we can have right now, if only we see it and act on it.

Sadly, this over-realisation has led to some great hardships for believers. For example, some Christians have thought that, since they receive the Holy Spirit by having faith in Jesus, they have in themselves now the power never to sin again (a view known as 'sinless perfectionism'). Emphasising verses such as Matthew 5:48 ("Be perfect, therefore, as your heavenly Father is perfect.") they claim not to sin and believe that if they do sin, their salvation is in jeopardy. They have taken the down payment of our future perfection to be the whole amount. But the Bible contains plenty of discussion of sin in the life of believers, (e.g. Gal 5:16–26; 1 John 2:1). Many Christians have abandoned their faith because they were taught that unless they are sinless now, they have no place in God's kingdom. What a tragedy![8]

Another mistaken form of over-realised eschatology is more political in nature. Some theologians, excited by the prospect of God's justice arriving, have concluded that we can *bring about* God's kingdom by correcting injustice here on earth ourselves. This is sometimes called 'liberation theology'. Although the term is a bit dated now, it serves well to describe the emphasis on Jesus as a liberator of the oppressed. It often gains favour in areas of the world where large-scale social injustice is obvious and where many people are enduring terrible suffering while others feather their nests.

Such thinking moves away from a biblical view when it overstates the power of Christians to overthrow earthly rulers and bring about justice by revolution and social change.

However, we must say at this point that a proper biblical understanding that God's justice remains in the future is not an excuse for sticking our heads in the sand and doing nothing in the present! In fact, the opposite is true. Since we know that God will bring justice for all when he appears as our Judge, we should now be striving to be like him, to act justly, to care for the people that our Judge cares for, to make sure we are loving our neighbour as he commands. Knowing that God will bring ultimate justice means that our efforts now are worthwhile in the end. No despot or army can derail the coming kingdom of God. The ethos of liberation theology is surely correct—a society should be judged by how it treats its weakest members. But when this becomes an expectation that fairness and freedom for all can be brought about by the church's endeavours, then the Bible's view of Christian hope has been overridden.

A final version of over-realised eschatology is found in the 'healthy and wealthy' gospel of prosperity taught by some churches. In brief, these churches often emphasise Old Testament promises of God made to Israel and apply them to Christians today. For instance, in Joshua 1:8 the Lord teaches Joshua:

> Do not let this Book of the Law depart from your mouth;
> meditate on it day and night, so that you may be careful to
> do everything written in it. Then you will be prosperous
> and successful.

A prosperity gospel preacher might expound the passage using logic such as this: if we learn and obey God's word, we will prosper and succeed; to prosper means to be wealthy, and to succeed means to do well in life; therefore, God is promising that his obedient servants will be rewarded with riches and great stature.

It is true that God's faithful and obedient servants will be rewarded—but the New Testament tells us that this reward remains in the future kingdom. The preacher has taken a specific promise to Joshua, as God commissions him to lead Israel into the promised land of Canaan, and 'materialised' that promise into twenty-first century life. This is an abuse of the Bible and a misunderstanding of the hope that we are given in Christ.

Then there's the *health* part of this 'healthy and wealthy' gospel. John was recently in an overseas church where a preacher asked people with illnesses to come to the front for prayer and healing. No problem there, of course; the Scriptures encourage congregational prayer for healing (Jas 5:14–16). But then the minister asked if anyone in the church was feeling the effects of a creation 'groaning as in the pains of childbirth'. The reference was to Romans 8:19–22 where Paul says that the creation itself groans as it waits for liberation from its bondage to decay. Astonishingly, as people began to stand up with their various stresses, aches and pains, the preacher started 'rebuking' these evidences of creation's decay and claiming in Christ's name 'liberation' and 'new creation' right here and now. If only people had turned to Romans 8 they would have discovered that Paul says the liberation of creation is *entirely* future. Until then we can expect suffering before glory: "I consider that our present sufferings are not worth comparing with the glory that will be revealed in us" (Rom 8:18).

Such over-realisation of Christian hope does nothing to help a Christian live in this time before the return of Jesus. On the contrary, it belittles Jesus' coming reign because it turns human beings once again into their own source of hope—as political liberators, or self-perfecting saints, or Top 100 earners or health gurus. The New Testament teaches an even greater hope to come, but it must be ushered in by the source of the hope himself, the risen Lord Jesus.

Living now for the future

In summary, Christianity is three-dimensional: it is about faith in Jesus Christ, love of God and our neighbour and hope in God's promised future. And, while many contemporary Christians are good at 'faith' and 'love', too many of us are 'no-hopers'. We are two-dimensional. We ignore the third dimension of the Christian life, and miss out on the excitement and assurance of hoping for what has been made certain by Jesus.

For so many of us, *God's promised future* features little in our thoughts and prayers and ministry. Our youthful longing for Christ's return and for God's eternal kingdom have dwindled over the years.

Why?

Is it because we have matured and acquired a more measured understanding of biblical faith? Is it because we are embarrassed about being associated with those 'fanatics' who try to predict the hour of Jesus' return? Is it because we find the whole thing difficult to believe now after centuries have passed? Is it because we have so many friends who refuse God and about whose fate we deeply worry?

Perhaps all of these have contributed. But the main reason for this dulling of hope, we believe, is that over time we have grown unhealthily attached to *now*. We like where we live! We love our friends, good food and wine, television, music and travel. And even though we know there is untold poverty, tyranny and godlessness in the world, and that Christ's kingdom will make all things new—we still find ourselves comfortable with the way things are *for us*.

There is, of course, a healthy love of life born out of appropriately revelling in God's creation. But there is also an unhealthy love of the world, one that selfishly prefers our private moments to God's promised future. When life is good, our eyes seem to drop from our future hope and rest upon our current contentment.

One German theologian describes the healthy Christian life as similar to a child's experience of Advent, the four weeks leading up to Christmas. The expectation of Christmas Day, with its parties, presents and celebrations, fills the whole of December with Christmas meaning. We wrap gifts, put up decorations, write cards and invitations, and so on. These Christmas activities are not only *born out of* expectation; they also serve to increase our expectation. They inspire us—the kids, anyway—and make the whole Christmas experience more tangible and exciting.

The New Testament says much the same thing about the Christian life. We live in the 'Advent' of the great arrival of Jesus and his kingdom. And our lives are to be decked out with the signs of that expectation—with praise for the coming Lord, with perspective on life's momentary troubles, in generosity with our transitory wealth, in joy that there is more to life than the present and in prayer that pleads "your Kingdom come".

2 | How to 'read' the future

Wacky Christianity

Loving the present is not the only reason modern Christians sometimes avoid thinking and talking about God's promised future. Another factor is surely that interest in eschatology, in 'last things', has too often been associated with the wacky side of the church.

Recently, the *Sydney Morning Herald* newspaper took a swipe at fundamentalists in the United States who, like an increasing number of modern Christians, believe in the 'Rapture'—the name given to an event where Christians are beamed up to heaven supposedly exactly seven years before the Second Coming (more about the Rapture in the next chapter). Under the not-so-balanced headline "Blind faith is the new power base", Francesca Beddie writes scathingly of the rise of Christian fundamentalism around the world, especially of the eschatological kind:

> The Pope says Australia is a Godless country. I take that as a compliment. What use does the Antipodean state have for religion? Do we want to be divided like Ireland? Or too frightened to get on a bus like people in Tel Aviv? Or in constant vigilance for the Rapture? The what? I was talking to a 15-year-old Quaker in Washington. "It's what those Bush-loving Christians

believe in. The day the world ends and they are beamed up to heaven." He told me to look on the web. The Rapture nerds have a site where those who will be saved can organise to have an email sent to their sinner relatives left behind on Doomsday. How that'll help I'm not sure but, while they are still on this earth, it seems to offer solace.[9]

There are some sections of the Christian community who, far from ignoring God's promises about the future, are utterly obsessed with them, and find specific teachings about the future everywhere they look. They have developed a peculiar language to describe their understanding of the specific events that will form the 'end times'. 'Rapture', 'millennium', 'tribulation' and 'antichrist' are all features of a narrative of the future that many Christians believe tells us precisely how God will do things.

Why is it that some in the church are blinkered by the present, and others are overwhelmed by a search for a roadmap to the future?

How did the wackiness set in?

Interpreting the Bible on the future

Many Christian obsessions with the future are caused by a particular problem: the way people interpret the Bible. These days it is commonplace for people to say "I can interpret a text like the Bible to mean anything I like". When it comes to eschatology, some Christians act like this is true!

The Bible is not just one book, but a collection of different documents, written at different times and in different cultures. It is a library of teachings about God, about the history of God's creation (and particularly the nation of Israel), and about the person Jesus. In order to interpret the Bible, you have to work out how the parts fit together, what role they each play in providing a true portrait of God's truth. This is where the errors can slip in.

Whole books are written on how to interpret the Bible, but the two most useful and important concepts for our topic in this book are *genre* and *style*. The genre of a piece of literature is the kind of writing it is, the category it falls into. The style of the literature refers to the choice of language in which it is written. And certain genres often have a particular style. For instance, the genre of popular romance fiction is often a very sentimental style, with long detailed descriptions of clothing, scenery and people.

There are all sorts of clues in literature that indicate to us what its genre is.

For example, if we write the following...

Maka tu tala bon toe
Kala tu tala ban boe
See-see mendala boo bay
Meema ben kala soo say.

... you will have no idea what we mean (since we made it up, like any bored five year-olds might). However, you will be able to tell me what kind of literature we have written: it's clearly poetry, or maybe lyrics, or a proverbial saying. The rhyme pattern, the meter of each line (dada du dada du da), and the sing-song way you say it as you read all suggest to you what kind of literature it is.

And knowing that it is poetry or lyrics informs you about how to read it. You don't expect it to be a technical explanation of a medical procedure, or a summary of your tax debt, or a letter from your employer. That isn't the way such texts are written.

When you know the genre of a piece of writing, you can start to discern its likely meanings, and also have some idea about what it is *unlikely* to mean. All of this is important to us because when it comes to understanding the Bible's teaching on the future, particular genres are used. Here are a few of them:

Instructive writing

Some of the biblical material about the future is written as a teacher might write to a pupil. It is didactic, plain prose, straight to the point. An example is in Paul's letter to the Roman church, where he teaches that "Christ being raised from the dead will never die again" (Rom 6:9). This is a clear instruction that Jesus is alive eternally; if we discovered Jesus had died later on, we would know the teaching was incorrect. It's that straightforward. However, it may surprise you to discover that not very much of the biblical teaching about the future takes this form.

Imagery and imaginative description

Most of the New Testament material about the future is in the form of metaphors and similes—images of what the future will be *like*. Jesus compares his coming Kingdom with a whole range of images that his listeners would be familiar with: the kingdom of heaven is like "a mustard seed sown in a field", "a treasure hidden in a field", "a net thrown into the sea to gather fish". In 1 Corinthians 15, Paul describes being resurrected as like growing a plant from a dying seed *and* as like putting on new clothing—two very different images of newness. Over and again, the New Testament describes the risen Jesus as "sitting at the right hand of the Father", a metaphor for shared rulership and authority (or do you think the Father really has a right hand and Jesus is always sitting next to it?).

Images sometimes get a bad rap, as if they were a second-best way of communicating. We like it when people just 'tell us straight' rather than using pictures and metaphors. However, the fact of the matter is that this is the way the Bible tells us about the future and of how God's promises will be fulfilled. There is no point objecting to it; rather, we should relish it. Our task is to properly interpret the imagery to gain a true understanding of the things to come.

The way imagery is used in literature will tell us a good deal about how we are best to interpret it—and how we are *not to* interpret it. For example, in Revelation 12:1 we read: "A great and wondrous sign appeared in heaven: a woman clothed with the sun, with the moon under her feet and a crown of twelve stars on her head." We would be surprised if many (in fact, any) of our readers thought that a woman actually stood on the moon somewhere with the sun wrapped around her.

But this picture stills makes sense to us in our imaginations, and it communicates to us the splendour and awesome nature of the woman, suggesting cosmic royalty of some kind by the stellar crown. It is, in the true sense of the word, 'fantastic' because it is a fantasy that helps us to marvel at reality all the more. The reality is that great and wonderful things have happened and are happening in God's cosmos, and we are swept up into them.

It really isn't surprising that so much of the Bible's teaching about the future comes to us in images. After all, the glory and perfection of what awaits those who know Christ is something that, at present, we really can only imagine.

Symbolism

Slightly different from imagery, symbolism is a very important tool in the Bible's toolbox of communication about the future. All languages use symbolic words, numbers or phrases. Most Australians would understand the symbolic power of getting 100 runs in a game of cricket—it's just so much better than getting 99! And everyone knows the symbolic meaning of a red light seen at a traffic intersection. Symbols become second nature to us, and yet when we enter a different cultural scene, we become blind to their significance.

A few generalisations can be made about the use of symbols in biblical literature about the future:

1. Sometimes the Bible explains the meaning of its own symbols, for instance, in Revelation 1:20 where the writer explains precisely what his seven stars and lampstands symbolise: "The seven stars are the angels of the seven churches, and the seven lampstands are the seven churches."

2. Not all images are necessarily symbols. A man dressed in white will often symbolise purity or sainthood, but he could just be a man dressed in white!

3. Symbols are more than just disguises for a secret identity. They often play more of a role in letting the reader know where the story is up to. For example, the seven lampstands in Revelation 1 clearly symbolise the churches, but the most significant role they have in this passage is indicated in verse 13—Jesus stands "among the lampstands". Jesus is with his churches.

4. Some symbols that seem weird to us now (a many-headed beast, for instance) may have been commonplace to the original readers. We shouldn't assume that just because we find the symbolism weird, the text itself is too weird to understand.

5. Some symbols are used pretty consistently throughout Scripture. Some examples are numbers such as 7 (symbolising completeness or spiritual perfection), 4 (meaning everything in creation, as in the 'four corners of the earth'), 6 (meaning spiritually bad) and 12 (meaning a whole, united group of God's people, e.g. the twelve tribes of Israel or the twelve apostles).

6. When we are trying to understand a symbol, it is worth first looking to see if the symbol has been used in the Old Testament, in order to shed light on its significance. Much of the symbolism in the book of Revelation, for instance, can be traced back to Old Testament books such as Zechariah, Daniel and Ezekiel.

Prophecy

A standard biblical genre is that of prophecy. For understanding the future, it is a very important genre. Prophets in the Bible speak the words of God, often in warning of judgment unless the nation changes its ways, and sometimes in declaration of what God has planned for their wonderful future when they do repent. Many of the Bible's teachings about the future are given in the form of prophecy, declarations by a 'mouthpiece of God' about what is to come. In other words, they are direct revelations of God's plans.

All of the Old Testament prophets have plenty to say about what awaits Israel if it does not repent; and equally a lot to say about the wonders that will come if God's law is followed and his will prevails in the nation. But we have to be careful to read the biblical prophecies in the light of the Gospel of Jesus, for we are told that in the past God spoke through prophets (among other ways), but now, in these last days, he has spoken by his Son Jesus (Heb 1:1–2).

This cannot be emphasised enough, because many erroneous teachings in the area of eschatology are the result of someone reading Old Testament prophecy and not coming to terms with its 'complete interpretation' through the words and deeds of Jesus (Old Testament prophecies supposedly about the modern State of Israel are a classic example—but more about this 'Christian Zionism', as it is called, in the next chapter).

Apocalyptic

When it came to writing about the secrets of the future in the ancient world, there was no genre better suited to the task than the strange beast known as 'apocalyptic'. Apocalyptic literature was in its heyday between 200 BC and AD 100 (the New Testament, of course, was written toward the end of this period).

Apocalyptic was a kind of code language full of symbolic numbers, animals, colours and stock metaphorical descriptions of heavenly judgment and glory. The books of Ezekiel and Daniel contain some of the most obvious examples of apocalyptic writing in the Old Testament:

The mountains will be overturned, the cliffs will crumble and every wall will fall to the ground ... I will execute judgment upon him (Gog) with plague and bloodshed; I will pour down torrents of rain, hailstones and burning sulfur on him and on his troops and on the many nations with him.

(EZEK 38:20–22)

I looked up and there before me was a man dressed in linen, with a belt of the finest gold around his waist. His body was like chrysolite, his face like lightning, his eyes like flaming torches, his arms and legs like the gleam of burnished bronze, and his voice like the sound of a multitude.

(DAN 10:5–6)

Many other examples of apocalyptic literature can be found in the voluminous Jewish writings between the Old and New Testaments (e.g. 1 Enoch, 2 Baruch, Jewish Sibylline Oracles and in the Dead Sea Scrolls). But for our purposes it is important to know that Jesus and the New Testament writers were very familiar with this style and used it to great effect.

While parts of the gospels and the letters of Paul contain some classic apocalyptic statements, the most obvious examples are in the book of Revelation. The traditional name of this biblical book (in the ancient Greek manuscripts) is *Apokalypsis Ioannou*, the Apocalypse of John. Consider the following apocalyptic paragraph:

Then the angel carried me away in the Spirit into a desert. There I saw a woman sitting on a scarlet beast that was covered with blasphemous names and had seven heads and ten horns. The woman was dressed in purple and scarlet, and was glittering with gold, precious stones and pearls. She held a golden cup in her hand, filled with abominable things and the filth of her adulteries. This title was written

on her forehead: MYSTERY BABYLON THE GREAT
THE MOTHER OF PROSTITUTES AND OF THE
ABOMINATIONS OF THE EARTH. I saw that the
woman was drunk with the blood of the saints, the blood of
those who bore testimony to Jesus (REV 17:3–6).

While the symbolism of apocalyptic literature was well understood
by ancient Jews and Christians, it was completely foreign to Greeks
and Romans. And that was part of the point. You could say an
awful lot about your oppressors if no-one but the faithful
understood you. In the above passage, for instance, no ancient
believer would have missed the fact that the scarlet woman sitting
on a *seven*-headed beast represents the perverse power of Rome,
situated as the imperial city was on the famous Seven Hills.[10]

Apocalyptic literature has some common features that are
worth knowing about as we explore the Bible's teaching on the
future.

1. It often contains a 'heavenly' or 'hellish' journey for
its narrator, who goes to see what is really happening
in the realm of the spirits.

2. It usually contains symbolic writing and complex
fantastic imagery.

3. It divides history in half, the old evil age and the age
of renewal and goodness that is coming.

4. It divides the world into good and evil spiritual
powers (an attitude known as 'dualism'). It is very
concerned with good triumphing, with justice being
done, and with evil being punished.

5. It has a sense of inevitability about it—it declares what is to come, rather than issuing calls to repent or change the course of history.

It is easy to see why it is an appealing type of writing for a people under tyrannical rule! Apocalyptic literature offers certain hope for a future in which good will win, and evil will get its just deserts.

This brief outline of the genres and styles of biblical writing about the future should serve us well throughout the rest of this book. Keeping our eyes open to the kind of biblical literature we are exploring should help us to steer clear of falsely literal readings of symbolic passages, or of trying to pin down imagery for clues about dates and times and the identity of the antichrist when, in fact, it was designed instead simply to stimulate our religious imaginations.

With this literary education in place, what can we say then about a belief such as the Rapture or the Christian Zionism mentioned earlier?

3 | The rapture, Israel, and other Christian myths

UNFORTUNATELY, SOME MODERN believers are as baffled by the Bible's apocalyptic literature as the ancient Greeks and Romans were meant to be. As a result, they have been led down some interpretative sidetracks the original authors would never have predicted. By mistaking apocalyptic symbolism for concrete historical prediction, some of us have come to believe in some very novel ideas. Two of the best examples are the *Rapture* and the recent eschatologically-motivated political support of the modern State of Israel, otherwise known as *Christian Zionism*.

Does the Bible teach the Rapture?

Back in 1992 a small church in Sydney caused a media frenzy by predicting the very day and hour of the Rapture. The moment was set for 1 am Eastern Standard Time on Thursday, October 29. Sure, Jesus might have said "No-one knows about that day or hour" of such eschatological moments (Mark 13:32), but that was back then. Now, we were told, the Lord has revealed his apocalyptic calendar to Pastor Chang Hun Jo of the *Mission for the Coming Days* church in Gladesville.

Once the date was announced members of the congregation started quitting their jobs and giving up their possessions. The media camped outside the church waiting—waiting to publish the next ridiculing headline, which came soon enough, "No Sudden Vanishings in Gladesville".[11] If this were not so damaging (both to the sincere Christians involved and to the reputation of the wider church), it would be pretty funny.

The modern doctrine of the Rapture is based entirely on reading two *apocalyptic* texts in a *literal* manner. One comes from the Lord himself (Matt 24:37–42), the other from the Apostle Paul (1 Thess 4:16–17). On the basis of these two texts, a whole industry of religious storytelling has developed. Movies have been made portraying the horrific experience of returning to an empty family home because your believing kin have been secretly raptured (in 1970s America, the film *Thief in the Night* brought many a nightmare). Most influentially, pastor Tim LaHaye and writer Jerry B. Jenkins penned the recently-completed *Left Behind* series of novels and films. These novels tell a fictionalised version of the kind of Bible interpretation that we have been suggesting is off the track. And they have sold over 60 million copies of their books—that's a lot of misinformation!

In the *Left Behind* stories, the world's Christians are raptured, leaving everyone else behind to work out how to live in the countdown to Christ's return. Although they are fiction, they form the basis of many people's understanding of what the future is all about. And the Rapture is the key dramatic event that gets the story going.

Whether or not the series was successful because it tapped into what people already believed, or whether people were excited by the story and came to believe in it as the truth, we can't say. Historically, 'rapture theology' has a very short history, dating back to a forceful itinerant preacher called John Nelson

Darby in the mid-nineteenth century. Darby was fascinated by connections he saw between Bible prophecies and the philosophy of history. He thought he could divide up history into separate eras (called 'dispensations') to describe how God related differently to the world at each stage. Darby's most novel idea was that of the Rapture; before him, it did not feature in church doctrine.

Darby was convinced that Christ's return would be in two stages; the first would see the church raptured to heaven; the second would see the return of the heavenly church with Christ to win the battle for the earth against the forces of the antichrist.

Darby's view of the Rapture gained credibility, largely because at 1 Thessalonians 4 it was written into the margins of a new version of the Bible, The Scofield Reference Bible. A whole host of popularisers have followed, such as Hal Lindsey in his cult classic, *The Late Great Planet Earth*, the tele-preachers Kenneth Copeland and Jerry Falwell, and of course the *Left Behind* authors.

It is obvious that 'rapture theology' has had a big influence on Christian expectations about the future, at least in places where these books have been popular. We know of Christians who drove around with stickers on their car saying: "Warning: driver could disappear at any time". In fact, both of us spent many a teenage hour singing Larry Norman's apocalyptic classic, *I Wish We'd All Been Ready*, with its youth-group-chilling lyrics:

Two men walking up a hill
One disappears, and one's left standing still
I wish we'd all been ready.
There's no time to change your mind,
The Son has come, and you've been left behind.

So can this Rapture thinking be justified from the Bible passages mentioned?

The problem is: these two passages are not about a rapture in this sense.

In Matthew 24:37–42 Jesus is not talking about Christians disappearing while non-Christians carry on their lives as before. He is talking about the last day when he returns in glory to judge the world. His point is that on Judgment Day God will accept some and reject others. This will occur at an unexpected moment, right in the middle of normal business, just as in the days of Noah:

> MATTHEW 24:37–42. As it was in the days of Noah, so it will be at the coming of the Son of Man. For in the days before the flood, people were eating and drinking, marrying and giving in marriage, up to the day Noah entered the ark; and they knew nothing about what would happen until the flood came and took them all away. That is how it will be at the coming of the Son of Man. Two men will be in the field; one will be taken and the other left. Two women will be grinding with a hand mill; one will be taken and the other left. Therefore keep watch, because you do not know on what day your Lord will come.

The 'taken' and 'left' language has nothing to do with people being secretly beamed up to heaven while the world carries on as before. This is an apocalyptic reference to the judgment that will separate the world when the Son of Man appears: some will escape (like Noah and his family) while others will be condemned (as when "the flood came and took them all away"). And this will all happen while men and women go about their daily business.

The whole idea of the "coming of the Son of Man" (verse 39) is classic apocalyptic language. It is in fact straight out of one of the most obviously apocalyptic passages in the Bible. After describing a vision of Four Beasts, Daniel reports:

> DANIEL 7:13–14. In my vision at night I looked, and there before me was one like a *son of man*, coming with the clouds of heaven. He approached the Ancient of Days and was led into his presence. He was given authority, glory and sovereign power; all peoples, nations and men of every language worshipped him. His dominion is an everlasting dominion that will not pass away, and his kingdom is one that will never be destroyed.

The coming of the Son of Man to rule all the nations is a stock apocalyptic theme and whenever we see it in biblical literature we should be alert to the associated use of metaphor and symbolism—such as riding the 'clouds of heaven' in the Daniel passage or being 'taken' and 'left' in Matthew. There is no Rapture of the church in the teaching of Jesus, just a sudden, unexpected, world-dividing judgment.

The same thing can be said about Paul's supposed Rapture statement. 1 Thessalonians 4 has nothing to do with Christians disappearing, leaving non-Christians to carry on their business. The passage is all about the *last* day when Christ appears and the dead are raised for judgment:

> I THESSALONIANS 4:16–17. For the Lord himself will come down from heaven, with a loud command, with the voice of the archangel and with the trumpet call of God, and the dead in Christ will rise first. After that, we who are still alive and are left will be caught up together with them in the clouds to meet the Lord in the air. And so we will be with the Lord forever.

It is frankly amazing that this passage was ever associated with the idea of Christians being raptured out of the world prior to Jesus' public return. The first couple of lines make it perfectly clear that the appearance of Jesus isn't in secret: there are commands, angelic voices, trumpets and resurrections. And it is only 'after that', says Paul, that remaining believers, i.e. those who are still alive for the Second Coming, get to meet the Lord in the air. In any case, this is clearly apocalyptic language. The expression "caught up together with them *in the clouds*" recalls Jesus' return on a cloud (Dan 7:13, Mark 13:26 and elsewhere)—cloud riding is a symbol of authority in apocalyptic literature. Paul's point is that when Christ's judgment falls on the earth believers will not be dangerously underneath it; instead, they will be with the Judge on the 'cloud'. "In the air" just means at a safe distance from the judgment falling upon the world. There is no Rapture of the church in Paul's teaching. The idea is a Christian myth.

Is modern Israel eschatologically significant?

Our second case study in Bible misinterpretation takes us into one of the most disputed areas of church life in the world today—the place of the nation of Israel in eschatology. Rather than avoiding the issue, we hope that by exploring it we might go some small way towards alleviating the confusion.

Visit www.zionoil.com and you will find an oil prospecting company that operates in Israel. Their vision statement is this:

> From its inception, the calling of Zion Oil & Gas has been to assist Israel in the restoration of the Land by finding and producing oil and gas, the rock oil and

source of energy buried deep beneath the ancient hills and valleys of the Land of Israel, necessary to make the People of Israel politically and economically independent.

The founder of Zion Oil, Christian businessman John Brown, believes that God gave him a vision to play a key role in the restoration of Israel to its rightful place among the nations. God even provided Brown with a specific Bible verse about his proposed venture to take to Israel with him and to persuade financiers onboard:

> 1 KINGS 8: [41] As for the foreigner who does not belong to your people Israel but has come from a distant land because of your name— [42] for men will hear of your great name and your mighty hand and your outstretched arm—when he comes and prays towards this temple, [43] then hear from heaven, your dwelling-place, and do whatever the foreigner asks of you, so that all the peoples of the earth may know your name and fear you, as do your own people Israel, and may know that this house I have built bears your Name.

It's hard to argue with that kind of mandate!

But this is not a joke—Brown is serious, and he has the money to prove it. Brown is a Christian Zionist, a label for Christians who believe that the Bible teaches that Jews must return to their homeland from around the world, and that this new state of Israel will prosper and lead world affairs, before Christ will return. It is not a rare view: it is estimated that two-thirds of American Christians believe that the geographical state of Israel has a place to play in end-times affairs. It is usually known as 'premillennialism', but we'll leave the terminology discussion for a later chapter.

Such a view of what is going to happen springs from what

we consider to be a wrongheaded approach to interpreting the Bible. Christian Zionists read the Old Testament prophecies about Israel's restoration to glory and power, and apply them directly to the Middle East today. Take, for instance, this prophecy from Ezekiel:

> EZEKIEL 36:33 This is what the Sovereign LORD says: On the day I cleanse you from all your sins, I will resettle your towns, and the ruins will be rebuilt.

Christian Zionists insist that such prophecies must be fulfilled in our times, in the physical space of Israeli land, and that God (who always keeps his promises) will bring this about with the help of faithful believers. Strangely, Zionists often ignore the fact that some of these prophecies were in fact fulfilled when Jews returned bit-by-bit from exile in Babylon, as recorded in the Bible books of Ezra and Nehemiah.

The cause of Christian Zionists was escalated by events in 1948, when the modern state of Israel was established with the help of the United Nations. This was seen as the beginning of the end—the first time for 2500 years (since the destruction of Solomon's temple) that Jews would have a homeland instead of being scattered across the world. The Jews would return home and, in the view of some Christians, usher in the return of Christ. However, little thought was given to the first part of the Ezekiel prophecy above—it was repentance from sin that would bring Israel's restoration, and this was not particularly evident in the political machinations of 1948!

For Zionists, eschatological action will focus on the actual city of Jerusalem. There will be a holy war ('Armageddon', which we discuss in a later chapter), interrupted by a false 'peacekeeper' ('antichrist', often identified by Zionists with the

United Nations) who will betray Israel. Jesus will then return in battle mode, with the previously raptured saints, to defeat the enemy and convince the Jews that he is the Messiah.

Zionists then use the books of Daniel, Zechariah, and Revelation (and a few other choice passages) as a kind of 'roadmap' to the future of the world, particularly the Middle East. Some significant examples of this sort of 'literal' interpretation follow:

▷ It is said that Jesus the Judge will return to Jerusalem itself because Zechariah 14:4 prophesies, "On that day his feet will stand on the Mount of Olives, east of Jerusalem". An apocalyptic scene is interpreted as a preview of the historical event instead of an imaginative way of saying 'he'll come home'.

▷ The Beast of Revelation 13, a leopard-bear-lion mutant, is not a complex image of rebellion against God, but a specific code for an unholy weapons-selling alliance between China (a leopard is like a dragon), Iran (the lion used to be on its flag) and Russia (the bear).

▷ Revelation 9:15–16 predicts that there will be a major nuclear holocaust, since it says 200 million people will die and only nuclear warfare could kill so many.

▷ The number of the Beast, given as 666 in Revelation 13:18, helps us to recognise the antichrist. On December 2006, Dr Ayman al-Zawahiri, second-in-command to Osama bin Laden in his Muslim terrorist organisation, was 55.5 years = 666 months old. 2007 is his year to wreak terror.

> Pastor John Hagee, an end-times 'specialist', said, "Following Ezekiel 38, Russia will give military leadership to the radical Islamics who want to destroy the state of Israel and control Jerusalem ... That is the battle of Gog and Magog".

This is merely a sampler of the vast number of specific predictions that some premillennial thinkers draw out of biblical prophecy and apocalyptic literature. There is a common element to all of these predictions—they turn images and symbols from stories into predictions of fact. Once you have taken on board the fact that literature doesn't work like that—that an earthquake can evoke feelings of dread, or represent a loud noise, or be a symbol for a collapsing idea, and not have to refer to any actual earthquake—the idea of trying to work out which earthquake, when and where becomes ludicrous.

Attempts to fit biblical prophecy and apocalyptic literature into historical schemes are doomed from the outset and can only bring disappointment, mistaken identity and the demonisation of people we don't like (including authors who aim to debunk all this). Yet, so many Christians do believe in this way of interpreting the Bible's eschatological teachings and putting their eschatology to work. There are very strong connections between the Religious Right in America and pro-Israeli politics. During the 2006 war in Lebanon, Fundamentalist tele-evangelist, Pat Robertson, a very powerful figure in religious broadcasting, told *The Jerusalem Post*, "The strong US support for Israel in general is partially due to the Evangelical community." He directly links US military and political activity in the Middle East with the Bible's teachings about Israel.

We see how high the stakes are in interpreting the Bible

correctly when such large-scale political activities are affected by it. Bible reading (or, should we say, misreading) is dangerous business.

Part of the attraction of the 'current affairs' style of Bible interpretation is that it allows Christians to get involved with the end-times events that the Bible describes. As one Zionist organisation says, "Why just read about prophecy when you can be part of it?". It brings the Christian worldview to bear on global affairs—as if our gospel mission to the world was not enough!

The real tragedy of this misunderstanding of biblical literature is that it overlooks the magnificent gospel of Jesus. In their efforts to hurry Christ's return by supporting Israel economically and politically, Zionist Christians neglect the opportunity to promote the news about Jesus and the mercy and freedom his death and resurrection secures for the world. It is probably fair to say that many Zionists have lost their faith in the power of the word of Christ, and in God's willingness to change hearts and minds, and they have tried to take matters into their own hands. It's *Action-Man* religion, exciting but misguided.

America the weird and wonderful

Finally, a word needs to be said about America's peculiar prominence in the field of eschatological weirdness. Why has a literalistic interpretation of Scripture taken hold across America? The answer would fill many more books (and arises again in a later chapter), but some points can be made.

Firstly, America is what might be called a 'millennial culture'. It was founded on an ideal of how life should be lived, eventually expressed in the phrase "life, liberty and the pursuit of happiness".

America's great hopes for a 'heaven on earth' are encapsulated in city names such as Philadelphia (meaning 'brotherly love') and Providence. America is an experiment in ultimate dreaming, and some of those dreams end up pretty distorted and desperate once human sinfulness bursts the bubble of utopia.

Secondly, like many idea-driven communities, young America had a strong urge to expand. As the settlers spread out, they felt God-anointed to spread their optimistic lifestyle of human progress and ever-better technology. Over time, the idea developed of America as a 'redeemer nation', capable of pulling others up, and there was even talk of New York as New Jerusalem. These Christian terms shaped the way American public culture perceived itself. America is a nation playing in an eschatological key. And such terminology still creeps into the public sphere, as it did when the first US military operation in Afghanistan was named 'Operation Infinite Justice', before being promptly changed to 'Operation Enduring Freedom'.

Thirdly, America has a very high percentage of Bible readers. It's declining, but still 59 per cent of people read a bit of the Bible. This means that biblical ideas and language are much more part of the mainstream culture than they are in Australia. If that high percentage of people could move away from wrongheaded literalistic readings of apocalyptic and prophetic literature and obsessing over numbers and the identity of many-headed beasts to an eschatology sure of God's promises in Christ and patient with the progress of his gospel, that would be worth all the oil in Israel and beyond.

Reading the Bible on its own terms

Our point in this chapter is not just to debunk the Rapture and Christian Zionism—which, it must be said, are novelties in the history of Christian thought—but to underline the fact that the language used to describe the cosmic events surrounding Christ's return is usually symbolic and prophetic; and when we don't read the texts as they were intended to be read we do a disservice to God's word and to ourselves. The genre of eschatological discussion in the Bible is frequently apocalyptic, with its great appeal to our imagination. We therefore cannot insist on precision about the details of Jesus' coming or the Kingdom Come. We can know a few things for sure; the rest remains to be revealed.

We have spent a good deal of time in these last two chapters trying to make the point that in order to understand the Bible's teaching about the future, we have to learn *how* to read it. And if that required a short literature lesson and a little myth-busting, it will be well worthwhile as we come to explore other particular Christian concepts such as the millennium, the antichrist, and heaven and hell. It might help us to get our heads around what's *not* going to happen, especially if in our fiction reading, movie viewing and tele-evangelist watching, we have been stimulated to believe in ideas that do not come from God's word.

Which brings us back to where the chapter started, with a group of earnest Christians in Gladesville trying to work out what to do with themselves when they didn't get raptured. Sadly, they had burdened themselves unnecessarily with a doctrine that did not come from a reasonable and well-shaped interpretation of the Bible. If you have had a similar experience, and rapture theology or Christian Zionism has had a big place in your expectations about the future, we hope this chapter has given you a way to think again about whether these things are truly biblical ideas.

In the next chapter, we start to look more positively at a few things we can know for sure about the future. We begin with what is traditionally the first topic of a discussion of 'last things'—death.

4 | The personal apocalypse: a Christian understanding of death

Boxers can't punch it,
Nor critics dismiss it.
Don't knows can't not know.
The lazy can't miss it.

Governments can't ban it,
Or the army defuse it.
Judges can't jail it.
Lawyers can't sue it.

Scientists can't quell,
Nor can they disprove it.
Doctors can't cure it.
Surgeons can't remove it.

Einstein can't halve it.
Guevara can't free it.
The thing about dead
Is we're all gonna be it.

From *Death Lib.* by Steve Turner[12]

A philosopher called Fred Feldman wrote his book, *Confrontations with the Reaper*, following the death of his 16-year-old daughter from a long-term illness. After careful reasoning about the nature of biological death, whether death is evil, and why we hate death so much, Feldman concluded:

> So, though death looms large in our emotional lives, though we hate it, and fear it, and are dismayed by the thought that it will someday overtake us and those we love, we really don't know precisely what death is (p. 71).

Death is a mystery—What happened to the daughter he knew? Why did her body stop and her person 'disappear'? Can his dead daughter exist in any meaningful way other than in his memory?

These are powerful and painful questions.

As far as can be known, humans are the only animals who are aware that life heads inevitably and irrepressibly towards death. This burdensome knowledge tends to intensify worries about life, pressuring us to seek some purpose and rationale for existence. E. M. Forster, the contemplative author of *Howard's End* and *A Room with a View*, once said, "Death destroys a man; the idea of Death saves him". We want to understand what our lives are about, because death is such an affront to us.

For Christians, our understanding of death is gained through God's revealed word in the Bible, and we try to understand our experiences in the light of what God has told us; fortunately, death is a major topic in the Scriptures. And the unique hope of Christianity comes from our understanding of the death of Jesus.

In this chapter, we explore the Christian understanding of what death is, since it is a future that awaits us all. But before that, let's deal with some contemporary views of death outside of the Christian worldview.

The trouble with death today

Outside of Christianity people currently hold a number of views of death's meaning.

1. Death is meaningless

In the movie *Pulp Fiction*, a young terrified black boy is killed when a character's gun accidentally fires in the back seat of a car. The killer has no concern other than cleaning up the mess; in a perversely humorous way he says, "Oops!". The transition of this boy from life to death is about as significant as crushing an ant.

One possible view is that death is nothing much. People die every day, most of them insignificant to us and seemingly insignificant to the world. Their deaths are just part of the ongoing ebb and flow of time and space, without deeper meaning and without great consequence.

But this extraordinary position on death jars with most (have you ever met anyone who really deep-down believed it?) and is usually held in a strained way, as a theory about death rather than a heartfelt conviction. To most of us, life *does* seem meaningful, and death seems like a denial of that meaning. We don't want anyone's life to seem worthless to the point that their death goes unnoticed.

2. Death is purely biological

Ashes to ashes, dust to dust. The view that death is the end of consciousness is rather common these days. In this view, the human person is entirely described by their chemistry and biology. Death isn't meaningless, but its meaning is restricted to physical things. All the elements of what we call humanity—love, memory, storytelling, music, art, happiness, unhappiness—are merely by-products of chemical functioning. Death just represents the wearing down or sudden injury of the biological systems that are our bodies.

There can be no complaining about death when it is seen as natural and biological. It is just part of the way the world works. When our time comes, we simply must shrug our shoulders and accept the natural order of things. We might feel sad or angry or hard-done-by, when someone dies young or unfairly, but these feelings are simply part of our physical experience and have no greater significance than that.

3. Death should be laughed off

Human beings seem drawn towards treating death humorously. Stories abound in which someone is having a terrible time trying to get rid of a corpse; or think of the number of films there are which involve pretending that a dead person is still alive. It shouldn't be funny, but it is.

Humour normalises death. It makes it part of life, rather than a foreign invader. Humour also belittles death, something that suggests to us that we humans need to try to reduce death's power in order to cope with it.

New York Jewish film maker Woody Allen is the king of death-humour:

> "While taking my noon walk today, I had more morbid thoughts. What is it about death that bothers me so much? Probably the hours."

> "It's not that I'm afraid to die, I just don't want to be there when it happens."

> "Eternal nothingness is fine if you happen to be dressed for it."

"I don't want to achieve immortality through my
work... I want to achieve it through not dying."

Joking about death is one way of delaying its terrible impact on
us—while we are laughing, we can keep ourselves from crying.
We also turn death into entertainment in order to keep it at
arms' length. From the wide popularity of horror movies, to the
fascination with serial killers, to musical forms such as death
metal, we turn death into art forms that entertain us and keep
us remote from its reality.

4. Death unites us with the universe

A popular view at present owes much to the thinking of Eastern
religions, that is, that we are all part of the universe and death
simply returns us to our 'Mother'. There is, of course, some truth
in the idea that human beings are, as Moby sang, "made of stars"
and when we die we enter that great organism that is the universe
("for dust you are and to dust you will return" Gen 3:19). This
differs from the view that death is natural, because it encompasses
a great sense of meaning, since we all contribute to the Oneness
of the universe. In a sense, this view of death makes us like gods.

5. Death is the ultimate enemy

Since many people see death as the end of life today, it is also the
ultimate enemy. It must be resisted, avoided and delayed for as
long as possible, whatever the cost. We see this view applied in
our health system, where the lives of very ill or elderly people are
sustained far beyond what many people would describe as
functioning human life. British philosopher and theologian Paul
Helm wrote, "The modern western attitude to dying and death
is all too obvious. It is to avoid it, to avoid mentioning it, and

where mention of it is unavoidable, to use euphemisms and circumlocutions."[13] We want to avoid this enemy at all costs. There is something profoundly *un-Christian* about this naturalistic view. Death is not the end. The naturalist forgets that after death comes judgment. There is a fate worse than death.

A Christian view of death

In the face of today's views of death, what does Christian faith have to offer? The Christian view differs radically from all five contemporary views above. We think the Christian view of death offers great hope to those who fear death, who try to laugh it off, or who think of it as natural or insignificant.

The Bible teaches us four important truths, among the numerous references to death. Our hope is that you will let these ideas shape your own thinking about what awaits you and everyone else.

1. Our days are numbered

The Bible teaches that human beings have a lifespan set by God, and then they are destined to die. Human existence is mortal, and the best we can hope for is a long and prosperous life and a peaceful death. "Man's fate is like that of the animals;" writes the Teacher in Ecclesiastes, "the same fate awaits them both: As one dies, so dies the other. All have the same breath; man has no advantage over the animal" (Eccl 3:19).

But believers in Christ, though still mortal, die "in Christ" (1 Thess 4:16) in whom our life is hidden (Col 3:3). This is more like falling asleep than dying, such is the safety and security of dying in Christ. Those who die as believers are simply waiting for God to "give life to your mortal bodies through his Spirit, who lives in you" (Rom 8:11).

Since we know that death will come to us, we should prepare for it. One of King David's great psalms calls out for knowledge of when our end will come, so that we can be ready:

> PSALM 39:4–5.
> Show me, O Lord, my life's end
> And the number of my days;
> Let me know how fleeting is my life.
> You have made my days a mere handbreadth;
> the span of my years is as nothing before you.
> Each man's life is but a breath.

We mortals are to sort out our affairs while we can, while there is still blood running in our veins, especially our affairs with the One who can raise us out of our mortality into everlasting life.

2. Death is a kind of judgment

Although humans are created mortal, death is not our rightful end. The Bible teaches that death is a form of God's judgment. Romans 5 and 6 explore the way in which sin and death are entwined, the one resulting in the other. Death entered the world through the disobedience of Adam (Rom 5:12), a form of judgment and condemnation that was not just a one-off act from God but more like a curse that hangs over the world.

Death is therefore a form of punishment in which the creature designed to fellowship with God and revel in his creation, is separated from all such goodness. Humans are then radically degraded, having traded their birthrights for a bowl of soup, their immortality for material idols, becoming no different from the animal world:

ISAIAH 40:6–7. All men are like grass, and all their glory is like the flowers of the field: The grass withers and the flowers fall; because the breath of the Lord blows on them. Surely the people are grass.

The Christian approach to death is exemplified in Christ. Near the time of his death, Christ prays, "My soul is overwhelmed with sorrow to the point of death ... My Father, if it is possible, may this cup be taken from me" (Matt 26:39). Certainly, Christ had no death-wish; he desired to avoid the crucifixion if at all possible. He knew that death involved judgment. While Christianity is littered with martyrs, stony-faced or grinning as the flames of execution approach them, interestingly, their spiritual leader was himself so anguished at the prospect of death that he sweated drops of blood (Luke 22:44). The eighteenth century Genevan philosopher Jean-Jacques Rousseau once said, "He who pretends to look on death without fear lies."[14] Christ looked on death and did not lie. He knew death in all its horror. He knew that in his death he was taking on God's judgment for sin.

However, thanks to Jesus, the Christian doesn't experience death as a judgment. Death's power over us is greatly diminished. In John 8:51, Jesus says, "I tell you the truth, if anyone keeps my word, he will not see death". John Bunyan may speak of death as an icy river that pilgrims must cross in order to reach the Celestial City, but this may be an image of death best left in the pages of *Pilgrim's Progress*. Physical suffering in death can still be terrible for Christians, but there is no *spiritual* fear remaining in death, because Jesus has turned away God's wrath and removed the 'sting' of death.

3. Death is not the end, but ...

We will come to what lies *beyond* death in Chapter 10. That may seem a strange way to order our chapters but we think it will prove helpful. The emphasis of the New Testament is on the resurrection of the body not 'dying and going to heaven'. Eternal life, then, we reckon is best discussed not in connection with *our personal death* but as part of God's renewal of creation in the coming kingdom.

So, right now, we want to explore the very real sense in which death is final; it is a fullstop of sorts.

"Whatever your hand finds to do, do it with all your might," writes the Teacher in Ecclesiastes, "for in the grave, where you are going, there is neither working nor planning nor knowledge nor wisdom" (Eccl 9:10). Death brings to an end human endeavour, and what was left unfinished at death remains unfinished until judgment. Hebrews 9:27 tells us that humans are destined to die once (i.e. not to live multiple incarnations where they might finish off their plans or 'improve' their record), and then to face judgment.

This is a very difficult teaching for human beings to accept. We want to be given another chance, an opportunity to go back and fix up our mistakes or do something we left undone. Surely death is not such a dramatic and final end to the human account?

Tragically, a doctrine developed out of this desire to have another go at our past: the doctrine of Purgatory. As the name suggests, the doctrine of Purgatory posits a place or time in between death and judgment during which one's sins can be 'paid off' or purged by acts of penitence and self-punishment. This idea is associated mainly with medieval Catholicism, but continues to this day and has been a significant part of some Christian understandings of eschatology.

Frankly, there is not a line in the Bible that suggests it might be true. Although it might spring from such thoughts as God not wanting anyone to be lost (e.g. Ezek 18:32), there is nothing in the Bible to support the idea of a place of 'second chance'. The only possible passage on which to ground the doctrine is in the *apocryphal* book of 2 Maccabees (found in the Roman Catholic Old Testament). Here, a Jewish leader named Judas Maccabeus, an historical figure from the second century BC, makes an offering of money to atone for the sins of some Jewish soldiers who died fighting for God's cause:

2 MACCABEES 12:39–45. On the next day, as had now become necessary, Judas and his men went to take up the bodies of the fallen and to bring them back to lie with their kindred in the sepulchres of their ancestors. [40] Then under the tunic of each one of the dead they found sacred tokens of the idols of Jamnia, which the law forbids the Jews to wear. And it became clear to all that this was the reason these men had fallen. [41] So they all blessed the ways of the Lord, the righteous judge, who reveals the things that are hidden; [42] and they turned to supplication, praying that the sin that had been committed might be wholly blotted out. The noble Judas exhorted the people to keep themselves free from sin, for they had seen with their own eyes what had happened as the result of the sin of those who had fallen. [43] He also took up a collection, man by man, to the amount of two thousand drachmas of silver, and sent it to Jerusalem to provide for a sin offering. In doing this he acted very well and honorably, taking account of the resurrection. [44] For if he were not expecting that those who had fallen would rise again, it would have been superfluous and foolish to pray for the dead. [45] But if he was looking to the splendid reward that is laid up for those who fall asleep in godliness, it was a holy and pious

thought. Therefore he made atonement for the dead, so that
they might be delivered from their sin.

This story demonstrates the idea that believers who were
encumbered by sin could be 'purified' before entering heaven.
However, this is an apocryphal book belonging neither to the
Jewish Scriptures, nor to the Protestant Old Testament (which
contains exactly the same books as the Jewish Bible). The Bible
does not teach this view. Purgatory is a very human way of
trying to deal with a shocking discovery: that death really is the
end of a human life, and that judgment follows.[15]

4. Death will come to an end

In this world, death can seem endless. It is there every day, if not
in our own lives (if we are lucky enough to live in countries with
enough food, sanitation, shelter and peace), then on the
television every time we watch the news. It would be difficult to
believe that death itself will come to an end were it not taught
so clearly in Scripture.

Completely incapable of escaping from this state of physical
decay and spiritual mortification, humanity needs salvation and
finds it in the death and resurrection of Jesus Christ who was
"delivered over to death for our sins and was raised to life for our
justification" (Rom 4:25). Christ's sacrificial and voluntary death—
for he had not himself sinned—and his subsequent resurrection
brings about the death of death itself. Christ's triumph over death
is emphasised repeatedly in the New Testament:

> ROMANS 6:9. For we know that since Christ was raised
> from the dead, he cannot die again; death no longer has
> mastery over him.

1 CORINTHIANS 15:54. When the perishable has been clothed with the imperishable, and the mortal with immortality, then the saying that is written will come true: 'Death has been swallowed up in victory.'

2 TIMOTHY. 1:9–11. This grace was given us in Christ Jesus before the beginning of time, but it has now been revealed through the appearing of our Saviour, Christ Jesus, who has destroyed death and has brought life and immortality to light through the gospel (see also Heb 2:14–15; Rev 1:18).

Christian confidence in personal existence beyond the grave rests entirely upon the resurrection of Christ. It is not simply that Christ demonstrates that there is life after death; he had already shown this in raising Lazarus. The more important effect of Christ's resurrection is that sin has been accounted for, the death-penalty has been paid and the new creation has begun. In a wonderful paradox, the death of Christ has made death powerless.

Ignoring death threats

Death remains mysterious, terrible and unacceptable to us, and part of living the Christian life is to learn to cope with the threat of death and to remember that it is an empty threat. As Christians we lean totally on the work of Christ to undo death. And our belief that Christ has announced the death of death in his gospel sustains our hope that one day we will live in a world-to-come where death, the unstoppable tyrant, no longer reigns.

Meanwhile, in this life, we need to maintain a future perspective on death in order to overcome its threatening, menacing presence. All of us will face the reality of death at some stage in our lives. Our clear understanding that Jesus has done away with the power of death will be tested, and we will need to remind ourselves of death's powerlessness because of Christ. In the future kingdom of God there will be no more death, with its mourning and pain. Death will be swallowed up by life, as we shall explore in Chapter 10. Before that, we need to explore the event that will herald the transition from the old order of things to the new life of God's kingdom—the 'arrival' of Jesus Christ, otherwise known as the Second Coming.

5 | Ready or not: the future arrival of Jesus

DESPITE ALL THE WACKINESS and criticism associated with eschatology, there is no avoiding the fact, as stated in Chapter 1, that authentic Christianity has always been resolute in its hope. And a central feature of that hope in all mainstream Christian traditions—in Roman Catholicism, Orthodoxy and Protestantism—is the return of Christ in his glory, the so called 'Second Coming'.

The theme appears in the great historical creeds of the Christian faith. The Apostle's Creed (second – third centuries) says of Jesus:

> He is seated at the right hand
> of God the Father almighty;
> from there he shall come
> to judge the living and the dead.

The later Nicene Creed (fourth century), affirmed by all three brands of Christianity, declares:

> He will come again in glory
> to judge the living and the dead,
> and his kingdom
> will have no end.

More importantly, the theme appears in all parts of the New Testament: the writings of Paul, of Peter, of John and, of course, very often from the lips of Jesus himself in the Gospels. Eager expectation of Christ's appearance in glory is at the heart of a biblical faith.

Before we tackle some of the problems and misconceptions associated with the topic, please consider this summary statement of the Bible's teaching on the 'Second Coming':

> At an unknown moment in the future, Jesus—whose glory has been glimpsed in his life, death and resurrection—will appear in full majesty to judge the world, overthrow evil and establish forever God's kingdom promised in the Old and New Testaments.

While the Bible says this much plainly; some related issues are less clear.

Making sense of the prophecies

The first thing to say again, following on from Chapters 2–3, is that the language used to describe the return of Jesus prevents us from being overly precise about the details of his arrival—when, where or how.

This is true of prophecy in general. Take Old Testament prophecy about the first coming of the Messiah. We have to admit, some prophetic statements would have seemed a little obscure until read in the light of Jesus' fulfilment. For example, before Jesus entered into history it would have been pretty difficult to square the prophecy of Isaiah 11, which speaks of the Messiah's worldwide domination, with the prophecy of

Isaiah 53, which speaks of the Suffering Servant who achieves God's will through voluntary weakness and (apparent) failure:

With justice he will give decisions for the poor of the earth. He will strike the earth with the rod of his mouth; with the breath of his lips he will slay the wicked ... In that day the Root of Jesse will stand as a banner for the peoples; the nations will rally to him, and his place of rest will be glorious.

(ISAIAH 11:4, 10)

He had no beauty or majesty to attract us to him, nothing in his appearance that we should desire him ... By oppression and judgment he was taken away. And who can speak of his descendants? For he was cut off from the land of the living; for the transgression of my people he was stricken.

(ISAIAH 53:2, 8)

How could these prophecies possibly refer to one individual? Interestingly, confusion over Jesus' identity as Messiah was even felt by John the Baptist who sent messengers to the Lord asking, "Are you the one who was to come, or should we expect someone else?" (Matt 11:3). This is not to say the Scriptures are unclear; we are just pointing out that 'prophecy' is a different type of writing from 'history'. Prophecy usually employs images and speaks in the abstract. Historical narrative (such as the Gospels) usually offers concrete details in simple prose.

The point of this observation is simple. If the prophecies predicting the Messiah's entry into the *middle* of history were abstract and multilayered, we are probably right to expect that the prophecies concerning the Messiah's role at the *climax* of history will be equally so. Precision of interpretation just isn't possible.

There is an added problem with prophecies about Christ's return. Most of the statements about the so called 'Second Coming' are written in the literary style discussed in Chapter 2 called 'apocalyptic'. We must be careful about demanding to know too many of the finer details.

'Second' coming or 'arrival'

As we flagged in Chapter 1, the language of a 'second' coming is slightly misleading because it implies that Jesus' return is a follow-up visit. From the Bible's perspective the return of Christ at the climax of history is his *ultimate* coming.

The historical ministry of Jesus between 5BC—AD30 was not the main feature but the preview of the glorious arrival of the Messiah. It was the advance notice of who the coming Messiah is and what he stands for. It is only when he arrives in universal glory that it can be said that the Messiah has fully come in the sense intended by the Old Testament prophecies. This perspective can be found throughout the New Testament, once you know to look for it. To give a clear example, here is the Apostle Peter preaching to a Jewish audience in Jerusalem shortly after Jesus' death and resurrection.

> ACTS 3:17–21. Now, brothers, I know that you acted in ignorance, as did your leaders. But this is how God fulfilled what he had foretold through all the prophets, saying that his Christ would suffer. Repent, then, and turn to God, so that your sins may be wiped out, that times of refreshing may come from the Lord, and that he may send the Christ, who has been appointed for you—even Jesus. He must remain in heaven until the time comes for God to restore everything, as he promised long ago through his holy prophets.

According to Peter, there is a sense in which the Christ has not yet been sent. He has been glimpsed: yes; he has fulfilled the suffering prophecies: of course. But the full messianic work of 'restoring all things' is, as Peter indicates, still to come.

The same point can be seen in the default word used in the Bible to describe Jesus' return: it is not 'Second Coming' or even 'return'.[16] The word that appears throughout the New Testament is the Greek term *parousia*, which means 'arrival', 'appearance' or 'coming'. It features across a range of biblical authors:

> MATTHEW 24:27. For as lightning that comes from the east is visible even in the west, so will be the coming (*parousia*) of the Son of Man.

> JAMES 5:8. You too, be patient and stand firm, because the Lord's coming (*parousia*) is near.

> 1 JOHN 2:28. And now, dear children, continue in him, so that when he appears we may be confident and unashamed before him at his coming (*parousia*).

> 1 THESSALONIANS 4:15. According to the Lord's own word, we tell you that we who are still alive, who are left till the coming (*parousia*) of the Lord, will certainly not precede those who have fallen asleep.

It is no accident that this word, *parousia,* was used outside the Bible for an official visitation of the emperor. When an emperor appeared in a town with his massive entourage and all the appropriate pomp and ceremony, this visitation was called the *parousia*. The first Christians knew this well and made *parousia* the central term for the glorious arrival of Jesus upon the earth. It is probably in this context that we are to make sense of Paul's descriptions of Jesus' *parousia* in 1 Thessalonians 4:16–17 (quoted in Chapter 3) as involving 'shouting' and 'trumpeting' —typically imperial things. Paul is describing the arrival of the true emperor who has come to collect his due and establish his kingdom.[17]

The coming of Jesus at the end of history is his ultimate arrival. We have glimpsed his glory in his life, death and resurrection but it is not until his *parousia* that we will see the full extent of his majesty and mission.

Justice: the purpose of his coming

So what is the purpose of the *parousia*? What is the true emperor of the world coming to do? In short, he is coming to overthrow evil and establish justice.

It is no exaggeration to say that the central job description of the Messiah in the Old Testament is to right the wrongs of the world. Consider Isaiah 11, one of the founding messianic prophecies:

> ISAIAH 11:1–4. The Spirit of the LORD will rest on him—the Spirit of wisdom and of understanding, the Spirit of counsel and of power, the Spirit of knowledge and of the fear of the LORD—and he will delight in the fear of the LORD. He will not judge by what he sees with his eyes, or decide by what he hears with his ears; but with righteousness he will judge the needy, with justice he will give decisions for the poor of the earth. He will strike the earth with the rod of his mouth; with the breath of his lips he will slay the wicked.

In a sense, Jesus *did* slay his enemies with the rod of his mouth and the breath of his lips: his teaching overturned all that is false and opposed to God. But this is only a glimpse of his work of overturning evil and establishing justice. The real work is yet to come when, according to Revelation 19, which alludes to Isaiah

11, evil is destroyed by a weapon coming out of the Messiah's mouth:

> REVELATION 19:11–21. With justice he judges and makes war. His eyes are like blazing fire, and on his head are many crowns. He has a name written on him that no-one knows but he himself ... Out of his mouth comes a sharp sword with which to strike down the nations ... The rest of them were killed with the sword that came out of the mouth of the rider on the horse, and all the birds gorged themselves on their flesh.

Perhaps we can put it like this: the criteria of judgment was outlined in Jesus' earthly preaching, but the judgment itself—which will bring all things into conformity with that teaching—is still to come. And that is what the *parousia* is all about.

This is the point of the famous sheep and goats parable in Mathew 25 which describes what will happen in the Messiah's *parousia* and why:

> MATTHEW 25:31–36. When the Son of Man comes in his glory, and all the angels with him, he will sit on his throne in heavenly glory. All the nations will be gathered before him, and he will separate the people one from another as a shepherd separates the sheep from the goats. He will put the sheep on his right and the goats on his left. Then the King will say to those on his right, 'Come, you who are blessed by my Father; take your inheritance, the kingdom prepared for you since the creation of the world. For I was hungry and you gave me something to eat, I was thirsty and you gave me something to drink, I was a stranger and you invited me in, I needed clothes and you clothed me, I was sick and you looked after me, I was in prison and you came to visit me.'

This parable resonates with what Isaiah 11:4 said the Messiah would do: "with righteousness he will judge the needy, with justice he will give decisions for the poor of the earth."[18]

Preparing for the coming of Christ

If the purpose of Christ's coming is to overthrow evil and establish a kingdom of righteousness, we find here the key to living *in advance* of that kingdom. One of the dominant themes associated with the *parousia* is the need for us to live *now* in conformity with that future reality:

> MATTHEW 24:42–47. Therefore keep watch, because you do not know on what day your Lord will come. But understand this: If the owner of the house had known at what time of night the thief was coming, he would have kept watch and would not have let his house be broken into. So you also must be ready, because the Son of Man will come at an hour when you do not expect him. "Who then is the faithful and wise servant, whom the master has put in charge of the servants in his household to give them their food at the proper time? It will be good for that servant whose master finds him doing so when he returns. I tell you the truth, he will put him in charge of all his possessions.

The expression 'keep watch' (which really means *stay awake*) is not to be taken literally. Pastor Jo, quoted in Chapter 3, was asked by a journalist "What would happen if one were asleep or watching television?" (when the Rapture occurred). Tragically, he replied "You will be left behind. You must be prepared".[19] No. Jesus is simply using the metaphor of being awake to speak of activity in the Christian life. The second metaphor of the busy servant should make this clear. Jesus is talking about the need for us to be serving (God and neighbour) faithfully when he returns, for it is precisely that kind of loving service that will characterise the kingdom. This is the sense of the words "he will put him in charge of all his possessions". In other words, Christian service now is a sign and preview of our joyful service in the kingdom come.

Paul reflects the same idea in at least two passages; Christian living now pre-empts the life of the future. In the first, he is clearly reflecting on Jesus' words about the night-time thief quoted above:

> I THESSALONIANS 5:1–8. Now, brothers, about times and dates we do not need to write to you, for you know very well that the day of the Lord will come like a thief in the night. While people are saying, "Peace and safety," destruction will come on them suddenly, as labour pains on a pregnant woman, and they will not escape. But you, brothers, are not in darkness so that this day should surprise you like a thief. You are all sons of the light and sons of the day. We do not belong to the night or to the darkness. So then, let us not be like others, who are asleep, but let us be alert and self-controlled. For those who sleep, sleep at night, and those who get drunk, get drunk at night. But since we belong to the day, let us be self-controlled, putting on faith and love as a breastplate, and the hope of salvation as a helmet.

Notice the logic: we belong to the new day of God's coming kingdom, so let us live like the day is already here. And again:

> ROMANS 13:10–14. Love does no harm to its neighbour. Therefore love is the fulfilment of the law. And do this, understanding the present time. The hour has come for you to wake up from your slumber, because our salvation is

nearer now than when we first believed. The night is nearly over; the day is almost here. So let us put aside the deeds of darkness and put on the armour of light. Let us behave decently, as in the daytime, not in orgies and drunkenness, not in sexual immorality and debauchery, not in dissension and jealousy. Rather, clothe yourselves with the Lord Jesus Christ, and do not think about how to gratify the desires of the sinful nature.

There is a new era dawning with the arrival of the Messiah, an era marked by 'decency' and, above all, by 'love', and so we are to live *now* in anticipation of that time.

In a very real sense, Christian living is *future* living. When Christ comes to overthrow injustice, all that will remain will be peace, righteousness and love. Being awake and ready for that day means living by those realities now, letting the shape of the future determine the habits, thoughts and deeds of the present. There will come a day when justice will be granted to the oppressed, so we anticipate that time by living justly now. There will come a day when men and women will live together in absolute purity, so we anticipate that time by avoiding sexual immorality. There will come a day when peace will fill the earth, so we anticipate that time by fostering harmony in our relationships. And so on.

Our lives now are to be *living anticipations* of the glorious future of the Messiah.

The experience of waiting

One of the major threats to believers in the New Testament was the nagging doubt that Jesus might not return, as he promised he would. The apostles wrote frequently in their letters, reminding the early Christians that God would keep his promises.

The 'delay' in Christ's return obviously came to the attention of unbelievers, too. Those looking on at Christian faith might well want to mock Christians for waiting and expecting for so long.

> 2 PETER 3:3–4. First of all, you must understand that in the last days scoffers will come, scoffing and following their own evil desires. They will say, Where is this 'coming' he promised? Ever since our fathers died, everything goes on as it has since the beginning of creation.

The mockery and impatience for Christ's return continues today, and is powerfully depicted in Samuel Beckett's play, *Waiting for Godot*. Two tramps meet each other on the morning of a day just like every other day, in a barren wasteland, with just their boots, hats and a turnip to occupy them. Why are they there? They are waiting for Godot—or is it Godet? They can't recall. All they know is that they have to wait. He might come today (he always says he'll come today), but he didn't turn up yesterday. So they wait, and fill in the time.

It is an incredibly depressing (while at the same time very funny) play. There are two acts; they are nearly identical, and the play ends with the words "Let's go" and the stage direction: *They do not move.* They are still waiting for someone who seems destined never to arrive.

It can all seem so pointless, like waiting at a bus stop without a timetable.

Fortunately, the Bible gives us clear and compelling reasons for why God might delay Christ's appearance in glory. What we think of as 'wasted time', is from God's point of view patience:

2 PETER 3:9. The Lord is not slow in keeping his promise, as some understand slowness. He is patient with you, not wanting anyone to perish, but everyone to come to repentance.

2 PETER 3:15. Bear in mind that our Lord's patience means salvation…

JAMES 5:7–8. See how the farmer waits for the land to yield its valuable crop and how patient he is for autumn and spring rains. You too, be patient and stand firm, because the Lord's coming is near.

The passage of time apparently does matter to God, but in a different way from our expectations. Whereas we impatiently long for the end to come, God has a plan that is being fulfilled in his good timing, and it involves the salvation of many, because God does not want anyone to perish. These are comforting words for those of us who are yearning for Christ's return. And, in the meantime, we continue to anticipate the arrival of our King and his Kingdom, not only by praying "Your Kingdom come" but by embodying the words "Your will be done on earth as in heaven". Waiting for Christ's *parousia* is not aimless inertia; it involves living diligently as those who can see the first rays of the dawning New Day.

The Millennium

Now that we have passed the year 2000, everyone is familiar with the word 'millennium'. Previously, the word was mainly heard in circles of discussion that included the same people who were talking about the Rapture.

Views about the millennium separate Christians as much as views on the Rapture—and the two are connected. And both are connected with our understanding of the return of Christ, which is why here is the place for a discussion of the various positions that Christians hold. We do this a little reluctantly since, like the Rapture, there is little biblical warrant for taking up much time with arguments over the nature of the millennium.

There is only one Bible passage mentioning a thousand-year-period (a 'millennium'), and that is Revelation 20:1–10. In this exciting passage, an angel unlocks a place called the Abyss and hurls the 'ancient serpent', Satan, into it. The angel locks him in for a thousand years, so he cannot wreak havoc on the nations anymore. At this point, Christian martyrs are resurrected and reign with Christ as judges for the thousand years. After the thousand years have ended, rather like the end of a movie setting itself up for a sequel, Satan is released from prison to deceive the nations once more.

This is certainly a striking story—the sort of story you don't forget in a hurry, especially if you first hear it in your formative years. But why has it demanded attention from Christians such that churches have even split over their interpretation of its meaning?

Once again, we would suggest that a mistake has been made in biblical interpretation. Instead of seeing this passage as visionary, apocalyptic literature painting word-pictures about God's victory over evil, it is viewed as a coded revelation of the time line in God's mind. Because we don't think you can read this passage to work out what will happen when, in God's future, we don't want to spend much time on it. However, because it is so important to many Christians (in a way we hope to persuade them to give up!), we will outline briefly the three major positions held.

Amillennialism

Amillennialists recognise the symbolic nature of the term 'a thousand years', and believe that it refers either to Christ's complete reign of history with his resurrected followers, or sometimes to the period of time between death and resurrection (in other words, a kind of intermediate state). Amillennialists don't believe in an actual millennium, just some symbolic truth that evil will be brought to heel. If we had to place ourselves anywhere, we would both be here. Related to the Amillennial position is the Pan-millennial one that some of our friends insist upon: "Don't worry; it'll all *pan* out in the end!"

Premillennialism

Premillennialists do tend to believe in a literal millennium and that Jesus will return before it (hence, *pre*-millennialism). During Jesus' thousand year reign on earth Satan is contained. After this period, there will be a flare-up of evil, followed eventually by judgment day for the wicked. Premillennialists tend to be the most interested in dividing up biblical prophecies into specific indications of when God will do what. There are many subdivisions of premillennialism, some of which come up for discussion in later chapters.

Postmillennialism

Postmillennialists tend to believe that a real millennium will be experienced within history and that during that time the gospel will grow throughout the world, restraining evil and bringing peace. In other words, Satan is to be locked up for a special period of time *after which* Jesus will return for judgment (hence, *post*-millennialism).

It will be plain that we see little good in trying to sift out of the images of Revelation 20 a running sheet for Christ's return. And much harm can be done by suggesting that there is a 'real Christian' view on the millennium, and that you will only fellowship with those who hold it. This issue must not become a test of genuine faith.

There is a great message in Revelation 20 of the victory of Jesus and his risen followers over the forces of evil. Jesus reigns, and will continue to reign; and Satan will be defeated. Let us be content in that knowledge.

6 | Beyond 'Fire-and-Brimstone'

Getting away with it?

One of Greg's favourite movies is Woody Allen's *Crimes and Misdemeanours* (1989). The movie is a contemporary reworking of Dostoevsky's novel, *Crime and Punishment*, and both are concerned with the perennial question: can I get away with it?

In the movie, successful Jewish ophthalmologist, Judah Rosenthal has been enjoying his life to the full, including carrying on a long-term affair with a woman called Dolores. Unfortunately for Judah, Dolores has reached the end of her tether and unless he leaves his wife and marries her, she's going to spill the beans. Judah is faced with a dilemma—he doesn't want to leave his wife and his life of comfort and prestige. Then a solution is suggested to him. No-one would miss Dolores. No-one would even know she is gone. It will only cost you a few thousand. You won't even have to see the body. You'll get away with murder.

Horrified, Judah recoils from the idea, but only for a time. As the pressure of his situation mounts, he realises that, if there is no God to judge him, and if he's careful, then he just might get away with it after all. You'll have to watch the film to find out whether he does.

If there is no judgment of one's life, then Judah is surely

right. Nothing really matters, if our 'sins' can be kept secret from anyone who might care about it.

But very few people are happy with this conclusion. To start with, it just feels wrong to us. We *know* that our behaviour matters, and that injustice and evil ought to be corrected. In fact, we call out for justice to be done whenever we see horrible unfairness, such as in theft, rape or murder.

The idea that there might be no judgment—and that those who do evil might simply get away with it—leaves us sick in the stomach. Deep down, we all long for judgment to take place and justice to be done.

Most religions have some kind of teaching about judgment, be it karma (what you do will be done back to you), penitence (you'll have to pay your dues), or some sort of weighing of the scales of right and wrong. It seems that we human beings need to know that in the end, things will work out fairly.

Christianity is very clear that a judgment of human beings *will* take place. From the early stories of Genesis, we know that it matters to God how we act. God is so grieved with human wickedness that he condemns it in the flood of Genesis 6, rescuing only the household of the righteous man, Noah. This act of judgment weighs heavily on God, because his creation is so precious to him. Yet, he could not stand corruption and violence.

It seems that God's own heart demands justice, even at a very high price.

This leaves human beings in a dreadful situation, since we are all guilty in many ways. We don't even live up to our own standards of right and wrong, let alone those of a holy God. Scripture makes it plain that judgment awaits us. In the words of Ecclesiastes: "For God will bring every deed into judgment, including every hidden thing, whether it is good or evil" (Eccl 12:14; see also Matt 12:36; Acts 17:30).

The reality of the coming judgment is clear. It is on its way. There will be a day when we will be brought to account before God.

But what will the judgment be like? What do we know about the nature and basis of God's judgment?

Should the Bible's judgment language be taken literally?

What we said about Jesus' return needs to be said again about the theme of divine judgment: much of the Bible's talk on this topic is metaphorical, not literal. Consider these two statements from Jesus' lips about the fate of the wicked:

[They] will be thrown outside, into the darkness, where there will be weeping and gnashing of teeth.	They [the angels] will throw them into the fiery furnace, where there will be weeping and gnashing of teeth.
(MATT 8:11–12)	(MATT 13:41–42)

An outer 'darkness' or a 'fiery furnace'? Which is it? Unless we are to imagine a fire which emits no light, it seems best to conclude that these are images of judgment, not descriptions of it. Just as descriptions of Jesus' *parousia* employ the symbolism of the apocalyptic genre, so too do many biblical passages about God's final overthrow of evil. No doubt taking its cue from Jesus, Revelation 18 and 19 abound in symbolic pictures of judgment:

REVELATION 18:21–24. Then a mighty angel picked up a boulder the size of a large millstone and threw it into the sea, and said: "With such violence the great city of Babylon [Rome] will be thrown down, never to be found again".

REVELATION 19:11–15. I saw heaven standing open and there before me was a white horse, whose rider is called Faithful and True. With justice he judges and makes war. His eyes are like blazing fire, and on his head are many crowns … Out of his mouth comes a sharp sword with which to strike down the nations.

Will an angel really throw a boulder into the sea on the Last Day? Will the messianic Judge really ride a horse while slaying the wicked with a mouth-protruding sword? The answer must be, no. These are all potent images.

Even the biblical word 'hell' at its core is a metaphor. The word *gehenna*, translated 'hell' in the New Testament, was originally the name of a valley south of Jerusalem. It was called the Valley of Hinnom or to put it in the three languages of the Bible:

in Old Testament Hebrew, *ge-hinnom*;
in Jesus' Aramaic, *ge-hinnam*;
transliterated into New Testament Greek, *ge-henna*

The original Gehenna, or Valley of Hinnom, was infamous as the place where the ancient Israelites, under the direction of King Manasseh (600s BC) conducted terrible child sacrifices (2 Chron 33:6) and where, as a consequence, God through the Prophet Jeremiah said he would bring Israel to complete ruin:

JEREMIAH 7:30–33. The people of Judah have done evil in my eyes, declares the LORD. They have set up their detestable idols in the house that bears my Name and have defiled it. They have built the high places of Topheth in the Valley of Ben Hinnom (*gehenna*) to burn their sons and daughters in the fire—something I did not command, nor did it enter my mind. So beware, the days are coming, declares the LORD, when people will no longer call it Topheth or the Valley of Ben Hinnom, but the Valley of Slaughter, for they will bury the dead in Topheth until there is no more room. Then the carcasses of this people will become food for the birds of the air and the beasts of the earth, and there will be no-one to frighten them away.

This fire-filled, deathly and demonic Valley of Hinnom (Gehenna) became the ultimate symbol in Israel for God's apocalyptic wrath against human sin. Many Jewish texts between the two testaments develop this motif (e.g. 1 Enoch 26–27; Sibylline Oracles 1.100–103), but it is enough to note that by the time of the New Testament *Gehenna* (translated 'hell') has become the default term for God's final judgment, occurring no fewer than 12 times:

> Matt 5:22 ; Matt 5:29; 30; Matt 10:28; Matt 18:9; Matt 23:15; Matt 23:33; Mark 9:43; Mark 9:45; Mark 9:47; Luke 12:5; James 3:6.

In short, these biblical images of judgment, whether of fire, darkness, the weeping and gnashing of teeth or *Gehenna* itself, are all metaphors and are not to be taken literally. In fact, it doesn't make any sense to put them all together and say, "There, that's what hell will be like". We must not therefore demand to know precisely what the judgment will be like—how it will be applied, how it will be experienced and so on. We can know a few things for sure (e.g. it is real, terrible, eternal and avoidable); the rest must remain unresolved. Many problems arise when eager Christians try to make concrete what God has left pictorial.

To make matters more difficult for us, most of our images of judgment aren't drawn from the Bible (as they should be). Instead, images and descriptions from movies, art and stories have filled our imaginations since childhood, while throughout history, particular dominating stories or artworks of judgment have often distorted Christian understanding. How many of us hold an image of Judgment Day involving a muscular, noble-looking ruler on a throne suspended in mid-air, with trumpet-blowing angels flying around his head, singing figures lined up in neat rows in the clouds alongside him, and pestilent, tortured half-human figures lying below his dangling feet?

Such images come from incredible artworks by famous artists such as Hieronymous Bosch and Pieter Brueghel the Elder, or Michelangelo, whose painting of such a scene on the wall of the Vatican's Sistine Chapel is one of the world's most famous works. These works often draw on metaphors and images from the Bible, but their portrayal of these images make them concrete, as if they are showing us precisely what God will do, where everyone will sit, and how few clothes they will be wearing!

We need to identify where our images of judgment have come from. Are they a mish-mash of ideas from art and movies? Or have they come from Scripture? And even if they have come from God's Word, have we turned the biblical images into expectations of a literal future reality?

Judgment language is not to be taken lightly

Let us be clear. Metaphors are employed in the Bible not because the images are unrealistic but precisely because the reality they signify is so potent, so awful, that straightforward language is inadequate. Metaphors of judgment must not be taken literally, but they most certainly must be taken seriously.

We need to repeat this point, so that no-one is led astray by what we are saying: the images of judgment point to, and just hint at, its terrible reality. They may not be physical descriptions of what will happen in judgment, but they are powerful emotional impressions of what it will be like to endure God's judgment. God's judgment is real, and we need all of these horrific and overwhelming images in order to compel us to take it seriously.

Nowadays, people often reject any idea of divine judgment. Part of the reason for this could be a reaction to the 'fire and brimstone' preaching in some quarters of the church (or at least of the media caricature of such preaching). How many people have been put off Christianity by hearing sermons that appeared to delight in the condemnation of the non-Christian? Frankly, we have both winced more than once as we listened to some fresh-faced preacher speak of God's punishment of the ungodly the way we might speak of Australia's 5–0 white-wash of the English in the 2007 Ashes series.

Another reason society recoils from the concept of God's judgment: we just do not like it. Sceptics can mock the Christian doctrine of hell all they like but, the reality is, beneath the patronising talk of judgment as 'medieval' and 'fear-mongering' lies the simple fact, rarely admitted, that such people *prefer* a notion of deity that affirms more than judges, fulfills more than rectifies. The inconvenient idea of a God who is unhappy with our way of life is a powerful motivator to exclude such a 'god' from our thinking. It is not that a God like this is inherently implausible (quite the opposite—we want a fair God); it is just that it does not suit our Western, individualistic, comfort-obsessed preferences to think of God judging us.

Furthermore, we tend to be very short-sighted and suffer a failure of imagination about judgment. We 'forget' that we care about right and wrong, and that we ought to fear the condemnation of the one who created us. The novelist George Orwell once observed sarcastically, "Most Christians profess to believe in Hell. Yet have you ever met a Christian who seemed as afraid of Hell as he was of cancer?"[20] The troubles of this world can seem all-encompassing such that we forget that a day of judgment awaits us. Even more so, the temptations and selfish pleasures of this world—what we can get away with—seem all-consuming such that we work very hard to forget that we will be brought to account for our sins.

But those of us who want to be guided by Christ rather than by our own preferences or blindspots have to resist this mental sleight of hand. We have to learn to see things Christ's way. And, once we decide to do that, we are confronted by the fact that Jesus regularly and without apology emphasised the seriousness of God's judgment. Indeed, one of the Bible's well-kept secrets is that the person most vocal about divine judgment is not the Prophet Jeremiah or the Apostle Paul but the Jesus of the Gospels. Of the twelve New Testament references to 'hell' (*Gehenna*) cited earlier, eleven come from the lips of Jesus. The remaining one comes from the Lord's brother, James (Jas 3:6).

To dismiss, ignore or soften the idea of God's final judgment is to depart from a key element of what Jesus taught and who he claimed to be—which leads us to our next point about divine punishment.

Jesus as the agent of divine judgment

Throughout the Old and New Testaments the person most associated with the overthrow of evil and the establishment of the good is the Messiah. We have already explored the foundational messianic prophecy of Isaiah 11:1–4 where it is said that the coming king will judge the world, bring justice for the poor and strike the wicked with the rod of his mouth and breath of his lips. This passage appears to lie behind not only the parable of the Sheep and the Goats (Matt 25:31–46) but also the grand apocalyptic scene of Christ's coming in Revelation 19:

> REVELATION 19:11–15. I saw heaven standing open and there before me was a white horse, whose rider is called Faithful and True. With justice he judges and makes war. His eyes are like blazing fire, and on his head are many crowns. He has a name written on him that no-one knows but he himself. He is dressed in a robe dipped in blood, and his name is the Word of God. The armies of heaven were following him, riding on white horses and dressed in fine linen, white and clean. Out of his mouth comes a sharp sword with which to strike down the nations. "He will rule them with an iron sceptre." He treads the winepress of the fury of the wrath of God Almighty.

In some ways it is a comfort to know that the agent of future judgment is none other than the One who gave his life so that we might be forgiven. At the same time, it should give us pause to know that the One who will 'separate the sheep from the goats' and 'tread the winepress of God's wrath' is the same One who railed against greed and self-righteousness and who demanded we love God with all our heart and our neighbour as ourselves (Matt 22:34–40).

All of this highlights something about God's judgment which sounds obvious at first but which has implications that are rarely considered in some Christian circles.

God's judgment is 'according to deeds'

God will judge the world on the basis of human behaviour, in other words, 'according to deeds'. As Paul says in his letter to the Romans:

> ROMANS 2:5–6. But because of your stubbornness and your unrepentant heart, you are storing up wrath against yourself for the day of God's wrath, when his righteous judgment will be revealed. God "will give to each person according to what he has done" [a quotation from Psalm 62:12].

This statement is fascinating because it contradicts the common misconception that God's punishment of sinners will be applied *equally* to all, as if a Hitler-figure, to use an admittedly clichéd example, will receive the same judgment as a non-Christian humanitarian worker. We venture to say that this is *not* what the Scriptures teach.

It is true that any sin makes us guilty before God. As the Apostle John said, "Everyone who sins breaks the law; in fact, sin is lawlessness" (1 John 3:4). So, in one sense, *all sin is sin*. However, this is little different from saying that all crimes are illegal and make one guilty before the law. The statement is true but no-one would reason on this basis that therefore *all crimes are equal*, deserving of the same punishment. No; justice demands that some crimes be punished more severely than others. In a similar way, the Bible can affirm *both* that all sin makes us guilty before God and that some sinners will receive greater punishment than others.

In the above passage Paul quotes Psalm 62:12 saying that God's judgment is "*according* to what each has done". This does not mean 'because of' what each has done; it means 'commensurate with' or 'in proportion to' what each has done. The Apostle emphasises the point by talking about "*storing up wrath* against yourself". 'Storing up' (*thēsaurizō*) is a financial term, meaning to *amass* or *accumulate*. In other words, God's wrath against an individual can be lesser or greater depending on what s/he has done in life.

This does not for a second mean that good deeds can *avert* God's judgment or win his favour. Paul is adamant that "all have sinned and fall short of the glory of God" (Rom 3:23). The point is simply that, whereas salvation is independent of our works (on account of the fact that no-one is good enough to merit God's mercy), judgment is entirely dependent on our works because God is just. The Creator will give to each person in proportion to what they have done.

If you've never thought about it before, this may sound like a novel idea based on the nuances of a single Greek word. But many other biblical texts affirm God's proportional judgment. And who better to turn to than the future Judge himself.

Jesus contrasts the judgment due to some Jewish towns with the judgment due to some famously immoral Gentile cities:

MATTHEW 11:21–24. Woe to you, Korazin! Woe to you, Bethsaida! If the miracles that were performed in you had been performed in Tyre and Sidon, they would have repented long ago in sackcloth and ashes. But I tell you, it will be *more bearable* for Tyre and Sidon on the day of judgment *than for you*. And you, Capernaum, will you be lifted up to the skies? No, you will go down to the depths. If the miracles that were performed in you had been performed in Sodom, it would have remained to this day. But I tell you that it will be *more bearable* for Sodom on the day of judgment *than for you.*

It's worth pausing to reflect on this for a moment: the Lord said that the Day of Judgment will be 'more bearable' for some than for others—and in case we missed the point, he says it twice. God's judgment is not one-size-fits-all.

Or, again, in Luke 12 Jesus contrasts the judgment due to sinners who *know* his teaching with the judgment due to those who don't:

> LUKE 12:47–48. That servant who knows his master's will and does not get ready or does not do what his master wants will be beaten with *many blows*. But the one who does not know and does things deserving punishment will be beaten with *few blows*. From everyone who has been given much, *much will be demanded*; and from the one who has been entrusted with much, *much more will be asked.*

And, finally, speaking of the religious teachers of his day, Jesus declared:

> LUKE 20:46–47 (NRSV[21]). Beware of the scribes, who like to walk around in long robes, and love to be greeted with respect in the marketplaces, and to have the best seats in the synagogues and places of honour at banquets. [47] They devour widows' houses and for the sake of appearance say long prayers. They will receive the *greater* condemnation.

Those who have done the things listed here by Jesus will receive greater punishment than those who have not practised such hypocrisies. The point is clear: God's judgment is in proportion to our deeds.

Again, good deeds cannot avert God's judgment or win his salvation but the Bible does teach that, while salvation is a gift independent of our deeds, final judgment is not. God's punishment of the wicked is commensurate with their behaviour because God is just.

The point of this observation is to know that God's judgment will not be arbitrary—one blanket punishment for all sinners. Rather, it will be measured, appropriate and just. We have no idea *how* sinners' experiences of *Gehenna* could differ 'according to what each has done' but we have no doubt that it will. Some will receive 'many blows' and others 'few'. God's Word affirms it; God's justice guarantees it.

Pondering judgment

The theme of judgment will continue in the next couple of chapters as we explore what the Bible says about *who* are the main targets of God's coming wrath. In the final chapter we will discuss the topic of judgment of Christians. The reason for leaving this topic to the end will become clear. For now, though, we want to end with some very simple reflections.

How seriously do you take God's judgment? Do you find yourself so influenced by society's distaste for judgment that you ignore it, soften it, or even reject it? If so, we want to challenge you to allow Jesus' teaching to reshape your views. *He* is our Teacher: not the media, not our private preferences or our friends' opinions, but Jesus. The more serious we are as a follower of Christ, the more seriously we will take the theme of divine judgment.

Does your mental image of Jesus give due place to his role as the Judge of the world? This is one of the areas of real difference between the modern perspective and the perspective of the first Christians. They had no problem thinking of Jesus as both humble and glorious, both loving and just, both the Saviour and the Judge. In fact, it was precisely because they did think of him as the future Judge that they were so overwhelmed by the thought that he gave his life on the cross on their behalf. It is possible some of us need to recapture that wonder: we need to approach Jesus as the Judge of the world who, in an act of sheer grace, gave himself for us on the cross for our salvation.

Finally, the theme of final judgment should move us to praise God for his justice, a very common biblical theme. The fact that judgment is not arbitrary or capricious but entirely commensurate with each person's deeds should fill us with awe and thankfulness to God. The evils of the world will be put right not in a blind act of anger but in a measured, proportionate and entirely just manner. God sees all things, understands all the factors (mitigating or otherwise), and will apply his justice accordingly.

The longing through the ages that the Almighty would do something about the tyranny, violence, greed and perversions of human history will be satisfied on the Day of Judgment, as both victims and perpetrators experience no more and no less than is their due. It is this sense of God's proportional justice that leads the heavenly chorus in the book of Revelation to do what all Christians should be able to do:

> REVELATION 19:1–2. After this I heard what sounded like the roar of a great multitude in heaven shouting: "Hallelujah! Salvation and glory and power belong to our God, for true and just are his judgments."

Amen.

7 | The future of evil

"And in at the windows, and in at the door,
And through the walls by thousands they pour.
And down through the ceiling, and up through the floor,
From the right and the left, from behind and before.
From within and without, from above and below,
And all at once to the bishop they go.
They have wetted their teeth against the stones.
And now they are picking the bishop's bones;
They gnawed the flesh from every limb,
For they were sent to do judgment on him."

From the poem *God's Judgment on a Wicked Bishop*,
by Robert Southey.

ACCORDING TO LEGEND, in the tenth century in Germany there was a terrible famine in the area overseen by the Archbishop of Maine, a man called Hatto the Second. Hatto had gathered all the grain of the land into his silos, from where he could dispense them to those in need—that is, if he had wanted to. Instead, so the story goes, he invited all the poor to the door of a silo, only to lock them inside and set it on fire. He had found a great solution to the food shortage—burn the consumers!

It is unthinkable—a bishop dealing like this with "the least of them". Our hearts cry out for something to be done with him!

According to the legend (told in the Southey poem quoted above), the next day Hatto was besieged by rats, who chased him across land and sea until they wrought their revenge. The story goes that the rats were the souls of those whom he had burned, given the job by God of bringing judgment upon the evil bishop.

It's a legend (a popular one among people who feel oppressed by the Church!), but the lessons are clear. Such stories depend on the strong human desire for wrong to be punished; for the powerful oppressors to be made to feel what it's like to be on the other side of the gate; in short, for revenge. They also make a big call—that we could recognise a particular act in history as 'God's judgment', because it feels to us that justice is being done.

But is that true? How can we know when God is judging, by what means he is doing it, and who exactly is being judged for what? We saw earlier that Jesus is the judge, and that God's condemnation will be measured and just, "according to what each has done". Now we need to explore the when and why: when God's judgment will be revealed in this world, and why (in particular) it will fall upon the world.

Judgment now and then

People often ask about the timing of God's judgment. Does God judge here and now, in earthquakes, wars, rat plagues and bad-hair days? Or is the judgment entirely future? At different stages in the biblical revelation, different answers were offered.

In the early Old Testament literature—such as Exodus, Joshua, 1 and 2 Samuel—it seems that all of God's judgment was in the here and now. In Exodus 11 we see the punishment of the Egyptians; in Deuteronomy 9:1–5 we read of the punishment of the Canaanites; in 2 Kings 24:1–4 God punishes Israel itself. In all of these cases judgment takes place in contemporary events. We know this to be the case, because the Scriptures inform us God himself plays a major role in the events. He confuses the Egyptian charioteers and causes their demise; he drives out the Canaanites; he sends foreign raiders to punish wayward Israel. It is clear that these historical acts are part of God's act of punishment.

By the *end* of the Old Testament literature, however, the prophets are starting to speak about the 'suspension' of divine judgment. Whereas God formerly delivered his verdict within historical events, now he has fixed a day at the climax of history when he will overthrow evil and establish justice. In Old-Testament-speak, this was known simply as the 'Day of the Lord' (Zech 14:1–9; Mal 4:5–6). A particularly striking example is found in the Prophet Zephaniah (600s BC):

> ZEPHANIAH 1:14–17. The great day of the LORD is near—
> near and coming quickly. Listen! The cry on the day of the
> LORD will be bitter, the shouting of the warrior there. That
> day will be a day of wrath, a day of distress and anguish, a
> day of trouble and ruin, a day of darkness and gloom, a day
> of clouds and blackness, a day of trumpet and battle cry
> against the fortified cities and against the corner towers.
> I will bring distress on the people and they will walk like
> blind men, because they have sinned against the LORD.

By the New Testament period, this future 'Day of the Lord' is the default way of thinking about judgment. At this point, the Bible is explicit that, while God may still judge individuals through historical events (e.g. Acts 5:5–11; 12:23), he has in his grace suspended the Judgment until the end, giving people an opportunity to repent and seek his mercy. As Peter puts it so beautifully:

> 2 PETER 3:3–10. The Lord is not slow in keeping his promise, as some understand slowness. He is patient with you, not wanting anyone to perish, but everyone to come to repentance. But the day of the Lord will come like a thief. The heavens will disappear with a roar; the elements will be destroyed by fire, and the earth and everything in it will be laid bare.

If, however, people resist the offer of mercy right to the end, the warning is clear, both here in the letter of Peter and also in a statement of the Apostle Paul:

> ROMANS 2:3–5. So when you, a mere man, pass judgment on them and yet do the same things, do you think you will escape God's judgment? Or do you show contempt for the riches of his kindness, tolerance and patience [in delaying judgment], not realising that God's kindness leads you toward repentance? But because of your stubbornness and your unrepentant heart, you are storing up wrath against yourself for the day of God's wrath, when his righteous judgment will be revealed.[22]

In New Testament thought, then, in contrast to what is revealed to us in the Old Testament, God's judgment is still to come. This is not to say God never uses the events of history as punishment—we can be quite sure that he does from passages of Scripture as previously mentioned; the problem is, only he knows which events these are. From the New Testament's perspective, the judgment of God, crystallised in the images of *Gehenna*, is to be thought of as fundamentally in the future.

The Great Tribulation

There is a term that some Christians use about the judgment to come that we need to mention here. 'The Great Tribulation' has come to refer to a time in the future when the world will undergo horrific events and suffering unlike anything it has seen thus far. Depending on your particular brand of end-times thinking, the church may or may not undergo this tribulation along with the unbelieving world. Either way, it is considered to be a time of judgment prior to the final judgment—before the day of the Lord.

Expectation of a time of a great trial can be found in Old Testament writings such as Daniel and Zechariah, as well as in the Dead Sea Scrolls. The Tribulation would come before Israel was finally delivered from exile.[23]

The important passages of Scripture for those who think about the Great Tribulation are Matthew 24 and Revelation 7, read in tandem with biblical passages about the Rapture. Here are a couple of extracts:

> MATTHEW 24:21–22. For then there will be great distress
> [= tribulation], unequalled from the beginning of the world
> until now—and never to be equalled again. If those days
> had not been cut short, no-one would survive, but for the
> sake of the elect, those days will be shortened.

> REVELATION 7:14. These are they who have come out of the
> great tribulation; they have washed their robes and made
> them white in the blood of the Lamb.

There are a range of positions people take when interpreting these passages:

> *Pretribulationists* believe that Jesus will return secretly to
> rapture believers before the terrible time of distress and
> anguish on earth.

Posttribulationists believe that the time of suffering is taking place now for Christians (or will worsen in the future), and then Jesus will return in glory.

Midtribulationists believe that the church will be raptured somewhere in the middle of the period of suffering, after certain signs of the end have been revealed (e.g. those mentioned in Matthew 24).

Historicists believe that the church suffered these predicted hardships either during the destruction of the Temple in AD70 (strictly known as the *Preterist* view), or at least starting then and going on through the centuries to this day.[24]

All of these views read Scripture as a means of knowing in detail the events of the future. They all try to decode out of the Bible a series of events in a specific order.

What will happen during the Great Tribulation? The easiest answer is, "Read the *Left Behind* novels and the authors will tell you!" The views of those novels are firmly from the Pretribulation camp, and they capture in elaborate fictional detail the way these people turn the literary imagery of the Bible into concrete historical events.

Most of the 'glamour' players of Christian eschatology play a role in the Great Tribulation—the Antichrist, Armaggedon, the False Prophet, and the Beast whose number is 666. In fact, we would go so far as to say that many of the erroneous and damaging ideas people have about the Christian view of the future stem from this area of Pretribulational thinking.

Posttribulationism (and to some extent Midtribulationism) at least recognises that the Christian life in the here and now involves immense suffering (at least for some Christians) and that this suffering will be relieved when the Son is revealed in all his glory. However, Posttribulationism still falls into the trap of trying to locate particular historical events that indicate the Tribulation is taking place.

There is no complete and consistent schedule of events for the judgment at the end of time. Nor do the Bible passages about the Rapture, the time of distress, and the return of Christ all 'add up' to a single, clear set of future happenings that we could write like a history of the future. This is not the way the biblical literature is written. Many of the passages related to the subject are apocalyptic in style (Dan 7–12, Matt 24, Mark 13, Rev 7), and need to be read as apocalyptic literature should be read. They are exciting visions and imaginings of future realities, given shape by characters (such as the antichrist) and events (such as the return of Christ) which are meant to be received as revelations of the future in a form our imaginations can grasp.

The nature of the literature suggests to us that these events are meant to be understood not as detailed predictions of future happenings, but as images and stories of hope about our future, warnings about our struggles, and imaginative depictions of life to come before the day of the Lord.

Figures of evil

One of the most ridiculous evil characters of recent times has to be Mike Myers' megalomaniacal villain, Dr Evil in the Austin Powers movies. A parody of all arch-evil personae, Dr Evil wants to rule the world, destroy the moon, and be worshipped by all. He's a fool, but a dangerously powerful one.

There are literary figures of evil in the Bible, as well as actual historical figures whose lives were so evil that they became iconic representations of evil itself.

Christians run two risks when thinking about these figures. The first is that we treat them like Dr Evil, fanciful figures of fun who need not be taken seriously. And the second risk is the opposite: that we take them literally, as descriptions of actual people we are going to find in the newspapers. Three key figures worth discussing briefly are the Antichrist, the Man of Lawlessness, and the Beast.

The Antichrist is part of today's folklore, thanks to movies like *The Omen*. Mention the word to most people in the West today, and they will likely think of a film image of an incredibly wicked child, or a sickly pale man bearing a forced smile and wearing a black cloak. Alternatively, you may picture a world leader who has come to represent megalomaniacal opposition to God.[25]

None of these images help us in any way to understand the Bible's teaching on the antichrist. Somehow we have to rid our imaginations of them, as hard as that is.

The Antichrist is only mentioned by name in the letters of John, although similar opponents to God occur throughout the Bible. In the Old Testament, arch-evil rulers such as the Kings of Tyre and Babylon foreshadow the antichrist. Once again, the book of Daniel introduces such a figure, called the "King of the North" (Dan 11). He acts like a god and sets up his own religion in the place of true worship of God (just as the second century BC Syrian king Antiochus Epiphanes IV did when he erected a pagan altar in the Jerusalem temple). This is the figure to which Jesus alludes in the famous passages about "the abomination that causes desolation" (Matt 24:24; Mark 13:14). Interestingly, Emperor Caligula also hoped to place an image of himself in the Jerusalem temple; he died (AD 41) before being able to carry out the crazy plan.

The antichrist figure is sometimes an individual, sometimes a symbol, and sometimes a principle of evil. In other words, there is no one clear figure called the Antichrist. Instead, there is simply much opposition, personal and impersonal, to Christ. John summarises this state of affairs:

> 1 JOHN 2:18. Dear children, this is the last hour; and as you have heard that the antichrist is coming, even now many antichrists have come.

> 1 JOHN 4:2–3. This is how you can recognise the Spirit of God: Every Spirit that acknowledges that Jesus Christ has come in the flesh is from God, but every spirit that does not acknowledge Jesus is not from God. This is the spirit of the antichrist, which you have heard is coming and even now is already in the world.

> 2 JOHN 7. Many deceivers, who do not acknowledge Jesus Christ as coming in the flesh, have gone out into the world. Any such person is the deceiver and the antichrist.

The Man of Lawlessness has caused many Bible readers confusion. He is mentioned only in 2 Thessalonians 2, where Paul is discussing the return of Jesus with the Thessalonian church.

> 2 THESSALONIANS 2:3–12. Don't let anyone deceive you in any way, for that day will not come until the rebellion occurs and the man of lawlessness is revealed, the man doomed to destruction. [4] He will oppose and will exalt himself over everything that is called God or is worshipped, so that he sets himself up in God's temple, proclaiming himself to be God. [5] Don't you remember that when I was with you I used to tell you these things? [6] And now you

know what is holding him back, so that he may be revealed at the proper time. [7] For the secret power of lawlessness is already at work; but the one who now holds it back will continue to do so till he is taken out of the way. [8] And then the lawless one will be revealed, whom the Lord Jesus will overthrow with the breath of his mouth and destroy by the splendour of his coming. [9] The coming of the lawless one will be in accordance with the work of Satan displayed in all kinds of counterfeit miracles, signs and wonders, [10] and in every sort of evil that deceives those who are perishing. They perish because they refused to love the truth and so be saved. [11] For this reason God sends them a powerful delusion so that they will believe the lie [12] and so that all will be condemned who have not believed the truth but have delighted in wickedness.

There are almost as many theories about the identity of the Man of Lawlessness and the mysterious 'Restrainer' as there are words in this passage describing them. We don't intend to venture another hypothesis (though we both suspect the inventor of Disco is the musical Man of Lawlessness and U2 the great Restrainer!). What we will say is that the Man of Lawlessness is both a personal figure and a 'principle' or 'power' of lawlessness, the personification of forces of opposition to God. In fact, he deliberately seeks to usurp God's position. He is doomed to destruction at Jesus' glorious appearing. That much we can say for sure.

The Beast enters the biblical story in Revelation 13. It is probably just fractionally less famous than the Antichrist, but its number is more so: 666. What a distraction this has been for Christians! This symbol, while striking and thought-provoking, doesn't deserve the conflict and trauma that surrounds it. Like other numbers in Revelation, '666' is a symbolic mark which could be a numeric code for an individual's name (such as Emperor Nero), it could refer to a system of government, or it could be more broadly symbolic of an oppressor. It certainly doesn't warrant numerous hours with a calculator trying to come up with an algorithm by which to understand its meaning. What matters is whose mark you have: be numbered with the Lamb, not with the Beast. The Beast is an image of worldly power in Revelation, another force opposed to God and with designs on being god itself. With many heads, the Beast can hardly be thought of as a single person, but instead represents a greater force of opposition. For the first readers of Revelation the epitome of this blasphemous violent figure were the Roman emperors, particularly Caligula, Nero and Domitian who had rather ludicrous pretensions to divinity, but we don't need to look far in ancient or modern times to find countless other candidates worthy of the title 'the Beast'.

Summary thoughts

These figures of evil all represent opposition to God, and all come under God's judgment. Their presence in Scripture, admittedly sometimes difficult to understand, nevertheless has a very clear message for us—they will all be destroyed by Jesus the Judge.

If you have spent a good deal of your time worrying about the emergence of the Antichrist or the number of the Beast— please stop! You do not need to worry about such figures rising to power on the earth. Jesus Christ has won victory over evil in all of its forms, and you have nothing to fear. However, if you have never considered the power of evil in the world, the many people and laws and forces that work against Jesus and his gospel—you must give thought to such things.

It is pointless looking around for a particular historical Antichrist to oppose, but it is the very work of a Christian to be on the lookout for all manner of opposition to Christ, and to expect hard times and rejection and even suffering and violence when you faithfully promote Jesus as Lord and Saviour.

Do you see the distinction we are trying to make? Don't turn the literary devices into precise historical expectations; rather, use the powerful images and stories that the Bible provides in order to shape your conscience, your decision-making, and your understanding of the kind of genuine spiritual battle that Christians are experiencing every day.

8 | The three targets of God's judgment

Putting things right

WHEN JOHN FIRST became a Christian, he pictured God's judgment purely in terms of personal *morality*, as if God were the strict schoolmaster and we were the naughty children skipping classes, back-chatting teachers and 'losing' homework—there was no doubt a reason John thought of things this way!

But this 'morality paradigm' has the potential to blind us to a more basic perspective on judgment found throughout God's word. Judgment is about *putting things right*. It is about overthrowing what is wrong with the world and establishing what is good. Judgment is about condemning and punishing wrong, but it is also about remedying those wrongs.

We are not suggesting the Bible pulls punches when it comes to personal immorality; it doesn't. We need only to think of a passage like Colossians 3:5–6 to understand God's righteous anger against "sexual immorality, impurity, lust, evil desires and greed, which is idolatry." It is "because of these," verse 6 concludes, that "the wrath of God is coming" (similarly, Gal 5:19–21).

In this chapter, however, we want to highlight that personal ethics, as it is usually defined, is not the only—nor even the dominant—criterion of God's judgment. God is not to be thought of as the strict schoolmaster ensuring we all keep his rules. He is more like the heroic Justice Commissioner who vows to root out endemic corruption and expose all abuses of power. This 'justice paradigm' is stated perfectly in the description of the Messiah found in the foundational prophecy of Isaiah 11, quoted previously:

> Isaiah 11:4–6. With righteousness he will judge the needy, with justice he will give decisions for the poor of the earth. He will strike the earth with the rod of his mouth; with the breath of his lips he will slay the wicked. Righteousness will be his belt and faithfulness the sash around his waist. The wolf will live with the lamb, the leopard will lie down with the goat, the calf and the lion and the yearling together; and a little child will lead them.

Overthrowing evil and establishing justice and peace is the main business of the divinely appointed judge, the Messiah. Judgment is both a fearful thing (e.g. Heb 10:30–31) and something to look forward to, because God will do what is right and all the world will know it to be just.

So, what are the things God intends to put right on the Day of Judgment, his Day of Justice? We could be here all day looking up threatening passages about this or that evil, but we believe it is possible and helpful to identify three dominant, recurring themes—three principal objects of future judgment, three corruptions in the world that have to be put right.

The first has to do with the corruptions of human worship.

Idolatry: righting the corruptions of worship

From start to finish in the Bible God pledges to overthrow every human attempt to replace the Creator with *things*.

From the Bible's point of view 'idolatry'—the worship of a created thing over the Creator himself—is a perversion of our calling as human beings. It is a corruption of our office as those made in the image of God, made to reflect the rule of God in our service of him, the creation and each other.

There are countless Old Testament passages promising judgment on idol worshippers (e.g., Ex 20:4–6; 1 Kings 14:7–11; 2 Kings 17:6–20; Isa 2:6–9; Jer 7:30–34). Indeed, the exile of Israel in the eighth century is described as punishment precisely because of idolatry (2 Kings 17:6–11).

But this is not just an Old Testament theme directed at Israel's sin. The New Testament speaks with equal seriousness about the idolatry common to humanity:

ROMANS 1:18–25. The wrath of God is being revealed from heaven against all the godlessness and wickedness of men who suppress the truth by their wickedness, since what may be known about God is plain to them, because God has made it plain to them. For since the creation of the world God's invisible qualities—his eternal power and divine nature—have been clearly seen, being understood from what has been made, so that men are without excuse. For although they knew God, they neither glorified him as God nor gave thanks to him but their thinking became futile and their foolish hearts were darkened. Although they claimed to be wise, they became fools and exchanged the glory of the immortal God for images made to look like mortal man and birds and animals and reptiles. Therefore God gave them over in the sinful desires of their hearts to sexual impurity for the degrading of their bodies with one another. They exchanged the truth of God for a lie, and worshipped and served created things rather than the Creator—who is forever praised. Amen.

To raise the *things* of creation to the status of an object of worship is, in biblical thought, a kind of high treason. It is an unnatural and inexcusable suppression of the most obvious truth of all— that behind the beauty and complexity of the created order is a Creative Mind worthy of our praise.

There is of course a measure of idolatry in the major world religions today. But we must not be too hasty in assuming that idolatry is just, say, an Eastern problem. The Bible is clear that *any* devotion to created things in lieu of worshipping the Creator himself is idolatry. For example, Colossians 3:5 describes *greed,* i.e. the lust for possessions, as a form of idolatry:

> COLOSSIANS 3:5. Put to death, therefore, whatever belongs to your earthly nature: sexual immorality, impurity, lust, evil desires and greed, which is idolatry. Because of these, the wrath of God is coming.

Idolatry is therefore very much a Western problem (as well as an Eastern problem). The thought is terrible but there will come a day when God will find some of our friends and neighbours guilty of idolatry, regardless of whether they have engaged in exotic forms of religious worship.

Hypocrisy: righting the corruptions of religion

The second major target of the Bible's warnings of judgment is the religious hypocrite. There are plenty of Old Testament passages we could turn to (e.g. 1 Samuel 15:22–23; Psalm 50:1–23; Isaiah 1:10–20; Isaiah 66:1–4) but the threat of divine wrath against religious hypocrisy finds fresh expression as we revisit the statements about degrees of punishment explored in an earlier chapter. According to Luke 12:47, quoted previously, the person who claims to know God's ways and yet refuses to obey them will receive "many blows" compared with the "few blows" of those who don't know the details of God's laws. The same point is made in Luke 20:46–47, also discussed earlier, where Jesus warns that the hypocritical religious leaders of his day would receive "greater condemnation" than others on the Day of Judgment.

These passages are not an oddity. Readers of the gospels often note that the main targets of Jesus' 'fire and brimstone' preaching are not the sinners and tax-collectors, to whom Jesus usually extends the hand of mercy, but the religious hypocrites, those who name God as Lord but live as if he is not.

We should pause at this point and make clear that we are not talking here about the daily failings common to all believers. Those who try to love God and neighbour but do so inconsistently (and regretfully) are not 'hypocrites', in the biblical sense; they are just normal Christians for whom the pledge of forgiveness is never withheld. If you are someone with an overly tender conscience, please do not feel unduly anxious about the biblical indictment of hypocrisy.

The 'hypocrite' is the two-faced person, the one who puts on a show of piety but who blatantly defies the ways of God without repentance. It's the minister who continues in blatant sin while preaching about holiness. Or the bishop who doesn't believe Jesus is the Son of God. Or the respected church treasurer who steals from the weekly offering. Such people have a form of godliness, but deny its power, as 2 Timothy 3:5 teaches us. They can look godly without *being* godly. In this context we can be sure that the evils perpetrated by church members (and leaders) throughout the centuries—the Crusades, slavery, apartheid, child sexual abuse and so on—will be dealt with by God in a most severe manner. As Jesus said, such people "will receive the *greater* condemnation." On the Day of the Lord may none of us be found to be hypocrites.

It may also be appropriate to include within this category *those who reject the gospel*. Knowing the truth of God's will as revealed in the teaching, miracles, death and resurrection of Jesus (i.e. the gospel) and then rejecting it is a kind of hypocrisy. It is akin to the servant Jesus refers to in Luke 12:47 who "knows his master's will and does not get ready or does not do what his master wants". As Paul puts it succinctly: "He will punish those who do not know God and do not obey the gospel of our Lord Jesus" (2 Thess 1:8).

Of course, this immediately raises the question—at least, it does for us—of the fate of those who never hear the gospel, who never get an opportunity to learn the master's will. This is such a difficult subject that we have devoted the next chapter to discussing it.

Until then, we want to talk about a third major target of the Bible's warnings of judgment.

Oppression: righting the corruptions of society

Few things in the Bible receive more sustained criticism and serious threat of judgment than the treading down of the needy by the rich and powerful. Every bit as much as idolaters and hypocrites, oppressors will find themselves overturned on the day God puts things right.

The judgment of oppressors is a golden thread woven through the entire Bible. Why did God's judgment fall on Egypt at the time of Israel's exodus?

> EXODUS 2:23. ... because the Israelites groaned in their slavery and cried out, and their cry for help because of their slavery went up to God.

And what did God say to Israel as soon as they were delivered from this tyranny?

> EXODUS 22:21–24. Do not ill-treat an alien or oppress him, for you were aliens in Egypt. Do not take advantage of a widow or an orphan. If you do and they cry out to me, I will certainly hear their cry. My anger will be aroused, and I will kill you with the sword.[26]

And why, centuries later, was Israel in fact condemned to exile? Partly, as we have seen, because of idolatry and hypocrisy but also because of their oppression of the needy. This point is made over and over again by Israel's prophets. Some representative texts are worth quoting in full because the point is sometimes overlooked in our comfortable situation in the West:

> ISAIAH 10:1–4. Woe to those who make unjust laws, to those who issue oppressive decrees, to deprive the poor of their rights and withhold justice from the oppressed of my people, making widows their prey and robbing the fatherless. What will you do on the day of reckoning, when disaster comes from afar? To whom will you run for help? Where will you leave your riches? Nothing will remain but to cringe among the captives or fall among the slain.

Amos 5:11–24. Therefore because you trample on the poor and take from them levies of grain, you have built houses of hewn stone, but you shall not live in them; you have planted pleasant vineyards, but you shall not drink their wine. For I know how many are your transgressions, and how great are your sins— you who afflict the righteous, who take a bribe, and push aside the needy in the gate. Therefore the prudent will keep silent in such a time; for it is an evil time. Seek good and not evil, that you may live; and so the Lord, the God of hosts, will be with you, just as you have said. Hate evil and love good, and establish justice in the gate; it may be that the Lord, the God of hosts, will be gracious to the remnant of Joseph.

Zechariah 7:8–12. The word of the Lord came to Zechariah, saying: Thus says the Lord of hosts: Render true judgments, show kindness and mercy to one another; do not oppress the widow, the orphan, the alien, or the poor; and do not devise evil in your hearts against one another. But they refused to listen, and turned a stubborn shoulder, and stopped their ears in order not to hear. They made their hearts adamant in order not to hear the law and the words that the Lord of hosts had sent by his spirit through the former prophets. Therefore great wrath came from the Lord of hosts (see also Jer 21:11–12; Ezek 22:27–31).

And it is precisely in this context that the foundational prophecy of Isaiah 11:4 describes the coming Messiah as the defender of the needy: "with justice he will give decisions for the poor of the earth."[27] We have already seen how this messianic defence of the needy resonates with Jesus' parable of the sheep and the goats— "I was hungry and you gave me nothing to eat" (Matt 25:31–46). It is no wonder, then, with these words ringing in his ears, that Jesus' brother James years later would issue a similar warning about rich oppressors:

JAMES 5:1–6. Now listen, you rich people, weep and wail because of the misery that is coming upon you. Your wealth has rotted, and moths have eaten your clothes. Your gold and silver are corroded. Their corrosion will testify against you and eat your flesh like fire. You have hoarded wealth in the last days. Look! The wages you failed to pay the workmen who mowed your fields are crying out against you. The cries of the harvesters have reached the ears of the Lord Almighty. You have lived on earth in luxury and self-indulgence. You have fattened yourselves in the day of slaughter. You have condemned and murdered innocent men, who were not opposing you.

And, finally, can it be an accident that the New Testament's longest and most frightening chapter on divine judgment, Revelation 18, is all about the archetypal wealthy oppressor—the opulent, demagogic, tyrannical 'Babylon' (most likely apocalyptic code language for Rome)? To quote just a portion of this ominous biblical lament:

REVELATION 18:19–24. 'Woe! Woe, O great city, where all who had ships on the sea became rich through her wealth! In one hour she has been brought to ruin! Rejoice over her, O heaven! Rejoice, saints and apostles and prophets! God has judged her for the way she treated you.' Then a mighty angel picked up a boulder the size of a large millstone and threw it into the sea, and said: 'With such violence the great city of Babylon will be thrown down, never to be found again … Your merchants were the world's great men. By your magic spell all the nations were led astray. In her was found the blood of prophets and of the saints, and of all who have been killed on the earth.'

A dominant, though sometimes neglected, dimension of the theme of final judgment throughout the Bible is God's promise to put right the tyrannies of human history and individual conduct.

Viewed this way, the Lord's threat of judgment is much more than a theological scare tactic designed to make people more faithful (though there is certainly nothing wrong with such a threat from the living God); it is a kind of pledge to oppressed humanity that the Creator hears their cries for justice and will one day bring his justice to bear on every act of oppression.

Nor is God's pledge of justice applicable only to the oppressed amongst God's own people—the poverty-stricken and persecuted Christians of Sudan, for instance, or the marginalised and imprisoned leaders of China's vast underground church. At least two of our texts (Exod 22:21–24; Deut 24:14–15) make clear that the Creator hears the cries of the 'alien' (that is, the non-Jew) as well as the Israelite. And there is nothing in James 5:1–6 to suggest that the Lord's brother is speaking in anything but general terms when he refers to the 'workmen' and 'harvesters' whose pleas have "reached the ears of the Lord Almighty".

In this way God's judgment and compassion are two sides of the one coin. It is because God loved the unnumbered martyrs of the first century that he will bring the tyrannous Roman perpetrators to judgment; it is because he loves the downtrodden millions in Africa, Asia and elsewhere that he will bring to justice corrupt Third World regimes and neglectful materialist societies —or perhaps we should say, the *individuals* who contribute to such political and financial injustices.

The longing through the ages that God would do something about the violence, greed and corruptions of human history will be satisfied on the Day of Judgment, as victims and perpetrators experience no more and no less than is their due.

Fleeing the judgment to come

And so we conclude this theme with the plea to God's people that appears in the middle of Revelation's tirade against Babylon (code for Rome):

> REVELATION 18:4–5. Then I heard another voice from heaven say: "Come out of her, my people, so that you will not share in her sins, so that you will not receive any of her plagues; for her sins are piled up to heaven, and God has remembered her crimes."

Obviously, this is not a geographical plea, as if Christians were being told to leave Rome itself and find shelter in a holy huddle on the outskirts of the city. The plea is spiritual, intellectual and social. It is another way of saying "flee from the coming wrath" (Matt 3:7) or "save yourselves from this corrupt generation" (Acts 2:40).

And so we plead that all of us, in the 'Rome' of our day, *shun* the things destined for judgment, find safety in the mercy temporarily on offer in Christ and live now by the values of the kingdom that is coming. Let us say 'no' to every moral and doctrinal distortion of God's will; 'no' to the attempt in our culture to replace God with things; 'no' to the hypocrisy that so easily creeps into church life; and 'no' to the marginalising and neglect of the needy.

> REVELATION 18:4–5. "Come out of her, my people, so that you will not share in her sins, so that you will not receive any of her plagues; for her sins are piled up to heaven, and God has remembered her crimes."

9 | The fate of those who have never heard the gospel

ONE OF THE MOST difficult questions we are asked by sceptics is: Are you saying that all of those who don't know about Christianity are going to hell? The Christian speaker braces him or herself whenever the issue comes up in public. It is often asked as a red herring, but it is a very powerful one.

This is not just an 'apologetic' question; nor one of mere theological interest. It is probably fair to say that most believers at some stage in their lives have wondered long and hard about the fate of the untold billions who have never heard the gospel of Jesus. Think of the generations of indigenous peoples prior to European settlement of Australia and America, the great mass of Chinese people before the first missionaries, the countless civilisations of pre-Christian Africa and Europe, the millions in Islamic lands in our own day. Are they all, every one of them, lost for eternity?

This is an acute question, born of compassion and deeply felt by many, including the authors of this book. In the following pages, we offer a tentative outline of the main biblical themes that relate to this question. We cannot claim to have all the answers and we remain open to being challenged and corrected. We are keenly aware that it is a risky business trying to answer a question that the Bible doesn't even raise. Nevertheless, we hope our teaching flows not only out of a pastoral and apologetic concern but also, and especially, from a desire to sit under God's word.

With that said, let us launch foolhardily into this controversial territory.

The universal twofold obligation

The first thing to say is that no-one is going to be condemned to Hell for not having heard the message of salvation. Not learning the gospel is no sin, and the God of justice would never hold such a thing against a person (whether he holds individual Christians accountable for complacency in promoting the gospel is another matter—and one for another book).

But if failing to hear the gospel doesn't bring judgment, what does? In a sense, we answered this question in the previous chapter: God will judge the world for its idolatries (the corruption of worship), its hypocrisy (the corruption of religion) and its oppression (the corruptions of society). Obviously, someone who has never heard the gospel cannot be guilty of religious hypocrisy in the biblical sense, so that leaves two basic criteria: how a person worshipped and how a person related to others in society.

The point can be put more starkly. The Bible says there are two basic obligations on every man and woman. These bear down on us all as universal imperatives regardless of race, religion or culture. Human beings are to *revere their Maker* and *care for their neighbours*. These are the criteria of worship and society.

There are several ways we could demonstrate this universal twofold obligation throughout Scripture. We could note how Genesis 3 portrays Adam and Eve's sin as a defiance of God (fundamentally) and of each other (secondarily). We could also observe the way this rejection of God in Genesis 3 expresses itself immediately in Genesis 4 in Cain's murder of Abel, thus establishing a twofold pattern: when humans reject their Creator they begin to mistreat one another.

Then there are the famous Ten Commandments (Exod 20:3–17) which, as people often note, are 4-parts about honouring God (verses 3–11) and 6-parts about caring for other people (verses 12–17). Perhaps the clearest evidence of what we are calling the universal twofold obligation on humanity is the answer Jesus gave when asked to identify 'the greatest commandment in the Law':

> MATTHEW 22:37–40. Jesus replied: "'Love the Lord your God with all your heart and with all your soul and with all your mind.' [38] This is the first and greatest commandment. [39] And the second is like it: 'Love your neighbour as yourself.' [40] All the Law and the Prophets hang on these two commandments."

According to Jesus Christ, the central obligation of men and women is a simple, two-part directive: love your Maker and love your neighbour. The logic is seamless. If God exists, what could be more basic to human life than wholehearted devotion to our Creator and selfless care for our fellow creatures? There is no room left here either for the *religious hypocrite* who is zealous for God but uncaring toward others or for the *ethical agnostic* who aims to be nice to others but ignores the Maker himself. Both fail to heed the universal call of the Creator.

The judgment of 'those who have never heard'

This insight helps us to understand how God intends to judge those who have never heard the message about Jesus Christ. He will not assess their lives on the basis of something they don't know, but on something they do know: all of us must revere the Maker and care for our neighbours. In theory, it is possible to imagine someone in 'deepest darkest Africa' (as the cliché goes) who, though having never heard the gospel, looks at the physical world and at the human family and responds with reverence for the Maker and compassion toward others. Such a person would be 'safe' on the Day of Judgment—in theory.

The problem is, the Bible is utterly pessimistic about whether any human being, on their own, without the work of God's Spirit in their lives, ever responds rightly to this universal obligation. Instead, we reject these obligations. Even though in our hearts we know God's power transcends creation and that our fellow human beings deserve our compassion, we ignore the Maker (or fashion idols in his place) and mistreat our neighbours.

In his famous discussion of God's judgment on the world, the Apostle Paul makes exactly these two points. Firstly, men and women know the Creator's attributes but resist him. They break the first part of the universal obligation:

> ROMANS 1:20–21. For since the creation of the world God's invisible qualities—his eternal power and divine nature—have been clearly seen, being understood from what has been made, so that men are without excuse. For although they knew God, they neither glorified him as God nor gave thanks to him, but their thinking became futile and their foolish hearts were darkened.

At the climax of the discussion, Paul turns to the second part of the universal obligation. Far from caring for our neighbours, as we all know we should, we mistreat them:

ROMANS 1:29–32. They have become filled with every kind of wickedness, evil, greed and depravity. They are full of envy, murder, strife, deceit and malice. They are gossips, [30] slanderers, God-haters, insolent, arrogant and boastful; they invent ways of doing evil; they disobey their parents; [31] they are senseless, faithless, heartless, ruthless. [32] Although they know God's righteous decree that those who do such things deserve death, they not only continue to do these very things but also approve of those who practise them.

The point of this discussion is that we must remove from our minds the patently untrue (and unfair) idea that God would judge those who have never heard the gospel message *for not having heard it*. Instead, we should affirm that God will judge men and women on the basis of the things they *do* know. And everybody knows they should revere the Creator and care for those around them. On these criteria God's condemnation of the world is entirely just. As Paul says, "men are without excuse" (Rom 1:20).

Will God include sincere adherents of other religions?

At this point, we need to take issue with those who suggest that sincere adherents of other faiths will be saved on the Day of Judgment. In philosophy of religion literature this is known as Inclusivism, the belief that God will *include* some people from other religions. The view is certainly popular outside the church but it is becoming increasingly common within the church as well. The Exclusivist perspective—the belief that non-Christian religions have no power to save—just seems unbearable to many. We can well understand the point. As we have already said, few topics are more poignant and painful for the thinking Christian than the fate of those who have never heard.

Whatever the psychological attractions of Inclusivism, it seems clear to us that the Bible totally rejects any notion that sincere religious practice could remove the guilt associated with refusing to love God and neighbour. In any case, sincerity is a slippery notion. Do we include sincere witchcraft, astrology, Wiccan cooking, jihadist Islam? If not, why not? What additional criteria can we bring to the table to decide which sincerely practised forms of religion God would approve of and which ones he would not?

In our view the Inclusivist emphasis on 'sincerity' is a major departure from biblical theology. The Scriptures make clear that salvation from judgment has nothing whatsoever to do with sincerity of religion. One thing and one thing only averts the judgment men and women deserve for defying the twofold universal imperative—the atoning death and resurrection of Jesus. What saves is not religion (sincere or otherwise) but the grace of God in Christ, received by faith. We cannot emphasise this strongly enough.

We are left with three biblical facts relevant to a discussion of the fate of those who have never heard the gospel:

(1) All men and women deserve judgment for refusing to revere the Creator and care for their neighbours.
(2) Christ's atoning death and resurrection is the only basis for God's gift of mercy.
(3) God's mercy is promised only to those with true faith.

Is this the end of the discussion? We do not think so.

Restrained hope in God's mercy

Affirming the three truths above does not necessarily entail believing that God will save *only* those who confess Christ as Lord. Let us explain.

While it is true that Scripture has revealed one way of salvation, it does not follow from this that God will withhold his mercy from all who do not know that way. We must always humbly say with Moses: "The secret things belong to the Lord our God, but the things revealed belong to us and to our children for ever, that we may follow all the words of this law" (Deut 29:29). In other words, what God has revealed to his people is the truth and nothing but the truth, but it is not necessarily the *whole* truth. There are secret things as well. God would never contradict his revealed promises but he has the freedom to act in his world outside the parameters of what is revealed.

For our current discussion this means that God could, as an act of sheer mercy, choose to pardon men and women on the basis of Christ's atoning death, whether or not they knew about the means of mercy. Please note: we are not saying that God *will* pardon non-Christians on the judgment day, even less that it is possible to know in advance who such hypothetical people are. We are insisting on the obvious point that God *could* do it if he chose to and that, if he does, it will be on the basis of his grace secured through Jesus and not by any other means (such as sincere religion, good works, etc.).

We want to expand on this a little more and offer some biblical arguments which lead us to what you might call a 'restrained hope' that the Lord might extend his mercy to some outside the visible people of God—even though we remain fundamentally pessimistic about the fate of those outside of Christ.

How did God save pre-Christian-era Jews?

Will God have mercy on any Jews who lived before Jesus? The answer, of course, is yes. But on what basis will God forgive the sins of pre-Christian-era Jews? From the human point of view the answer is: *faith in what was revealed*. From God's point of view none of the objects associated with Israelite faith (circumcision, food laws, the sacrificial system and so on) had the power to save the sinner.[28] The basis of God's mercy to ancient Israelites was always the future atoning death and resurrection of Jesus. This is Paul's point when he talks about the unpunished sins of the past:

> ROMANS 3:25. God presented him [Jesus] as a sacrifice of
> atonement, through faith in his blood. He did this to
> demonstrate his justice, because in his forbearance he had
> left the sins committed beforehand [by Israelites] unpunished.

God was able to 'forbear' the sins of Israel's past because of the future atoning work of Jesus. Even though faithful Jews knew nothing of Jesus' sacrificial death, they were pardoned by God and granted righteous standing before him (Gen 15:6).

God's mercy toward ancient Israelites is easy enough to understand, and we are not saying that this is immediately relevant to the question of the fate of non-Jews who know nothing of Jesus. We are simply highlighting the fact that God is able to have mercy on people who have no explicit knowledge of Jesus' death and resurrection.

One obvious response to the direction in which we are moving is to say: "Whatever God's plan was for Jews before Jesus, we know that since the coming of Christ, salvation is available only to those who embrace the gospel. The year AD 30, in other words, was the cut-off point for God's mercy to Jews."

But can we be so sure?

Imagine a faithful Jew living in Babylonia in the year AD 35, decades before the gospel came to the region. He prays to his God and cares for his neighbours as outlined in the Law. His faith, in other words, expresses itself in humble obedience. Was such a man—as, indeed, there will have been many in Babylonia at this time—acceptable to God even though he knew nothing about Jesus *after AD 30?* Presumably, the answer is *yes*. Why? Because God was at work in this man's heart to produce true faith, just as God had worked in the hearts of all the Old Testament faithful. And such faith is always credited as righteousness (Rom 4:5).

This historical hypothetical is not intended to prove anything, but it does illustrate the difficulty in making a strict temporal distinction between Jews of the pre-Christian-era and those after Christ. The decisive issue is not so much timing—which side of AD 30 you live—but *faith* expressing itself in reverence for God and care for other people (the universal twofold obligation).

It goes without saying that if our hypothetical Babylonian Jew had heard the gospel, perhaps when visiting Jerusalem for Passover one year, and rejected it, his 'faith' would be shown *not* to be true faith after all. For true faith—faith produced in our hearts by God's Spirit—always responds rightly to God's revelation of himself, whether in the Torah, the gospel or in creation itself.[29]

Could God extend his mercy beyond the covenant people?

The obvious question, then, is: Can true faith ever be found *outside* God's visible people, that is, the people of the Torah (who did not know the gospel) and the people of the gospel? Put another way, does anyone ever look at the creation and the people around them and respond with true faith, revering God and caring for others? As we have said before, the Bible is utterly pessimistic that anyone *left to their own devices* ever does this. Sin rules in the human heart.

But that is not the end of it. There is no reason to think that God could not, as an act of sheer mercy, enable someone who has never heard the gospel to respond to the universal obligation with true faith and obedience. While such a person would be undeserving of God's grace, as we all are, they would nonetheless receive mercy. The basis of their salvation would not be their sincerity or good works but the atoning death of Jesus, even though their faith lacked the specific content of the gospel.

Please be clear about what we are saying. We are not suggesting that God always does this or even that he ever does this. We are pointing out that it is his perfect right as the Lord and Saviour of creation to "have mercy on whom he wants to have mercy" (Rom 9:18) and that, should he choose to do so, it would not contradict any principle revealed to us in Scripture.[30]

We remain pessimistic about the fate of those who have never heard the gospel. As we have previously explained, the coming judgment is as relevant to them as it is to the most strident, gospel-rejecting Westerner. God will judge us on what we know, and we all know enough to be condemned. But together with this biblical pessimism is a glimmer of hope, equally biblical, that the God of free grace might extend the reach of his mercy to some of our contemporaries who do not know the gospel. Let us explain where this measure of hope comes from in the Bible.

There are at least two examples in Scripture, one from the Old Testament and one from the New, of men outside God's visible people who appear to be acceptable to God without explicit knowledge of God's revelation in the Torah and the gospel. The first is the mysterious Melchizedek who is said to be both a pagan king and a priest of the true God, even though there is no biblical priesthood yet:

> GENESIS 14:18–20. Then Melchizedek king of Salem brought out bread and wine. He was priest of God Most High, [19] and he blessed Abram, saying, "Blessed be Abram by God Most High, Creator of heaven and earth. [20] And blessed be God Most High, who delivered your enemies into your hand."
> Then Abram gave him a tenth of everything.

There can be no doubt that Melchizedek's God is the God of Abraham (= Abram). More than that, Abraham's gift of "a tenth of everything" preempts the gifts Israelites would later give to the priestly Levites.[31] Abraham, in other words, recognises Melchizedek as a true worshipper of God. The story is strange on any reading but here, at the very beginning of the story of God's covenant people, we find an example of true faith *outside* of Israel.[32]

The point is simple: the fact that God has promised to bless the world *through Abraham* (Gen 12:1–3), and ultimately through Abraham's seed Jesus (Gal 3:16), does not rule out the possibility that he is able to reveal himself to some beyond the reach of the promise. We do not know that he *will* do this but there is evidence that he *can* and *has*.

Our second example comes from the New Testament. In Acts 10 we find the wonderful story of the first full-blooded Gentile to hear and embrace the gospel, named Cornelius. He is a Roman centurion, stationed at Caesarea on the coast of Samaria. But more interesting than his pagan credentials is Luke's description of him as a man of true faith acceptable to God. He is not a Jewish convert. He is neither circumcised nor living by the laws of Moses (as some former Gentiles did). But he is known as a man who reveres the Maker and cares for his neighbours:

> ACTS 10:1–2. At Caesarea there was a man named Cornelius, a centurion in what was known as the Italian Regiment. [2] He and all his family were devout and God-fearing; he gave generously to those in need and prayed to God regularly.

We might be tempted to wonder whether Cornelius' piety was simply a self-righteous attempt to win favour with the Almighty —the sort of thing we know God is not pleased with. But it turns out this fear of God and compassion toward the poor *were* pleasing to the Lord:

> ACTS 10:3–6. One day at about three in the afternoon he had a vision. He distinctly saw an angel of God, who came to him and said, "Cornelius!" Cornelius stared at him in fear. "What is it, Lord?" he asked. The angel answered, "Your prayers and gifts to the poor have come up as a memorial offering before God. [5] Now send men to Joppa to bring back a man named Simon who is called Peter. [6] He is staying with Simon the tanner, whose house is by the sea."

The reference to Cornelius' prayer and charity (i.e. his love of God and neighbour) as a "memorial offering" is fascinating because this is how the Old Testament describes temple sacrifices pleasing to God (e.g. Lev 2:16).[33] Cornelius belongs neither to the old covenant people nor to the new covenant people, and yet his prayers and gifts to the poor are as pleasing to God as a faithful Israelite offering. God has been at work in this man, granting him true faith expressing itself in love for others.

A common objection to this line of reasoning is that, if this were true, there would be no need to bring the gospel to such a person. On the contrary. In the logic of the book of Acts, it is precisely because the Spirit has been at work in this man that God is so eager to bring the gospel to him, so that Cornelius' faith might have its proper content, that he might be confirmed in the grace of God and that the Lord Jesus might be rightly glorified in his life. Far from being a reason not to take the gospel to him, Cornelius' status as one of God's people (along with all his household) is precisely why the Lord orchestrates a visit from the Apostle Peter.

Cornelius obeys the vision, another sign of his faith, and sends for Peter. When Peter arrives after making the 50 kilometre journey from Joppa to Caesarea he is amazed to find a crowd of eager Gentiles desperate to hear what he has to say. Before Peter explains the news about Jesus Christ (10:36–48) he says something of great relevance to the question we are exploring:

> ACTS 10:34–35. I now realise how true it is that God does
> not show favouritism but accepts men from every nation
> who fear him and do what is right.

To 'fear God' is to fulfil our vertical obligation toward the Maker, and to 'do what is right' (literally 'practise righteousness') is to fulfil our horizontal obligation toward others. This is exactly what Cornelius has been doing, according to verses 2, 4 and 22; the parallel is impossible to miss. Cornelius is a man of faith and obedience. He is therefore acceptable to God.[34]

To repeat what we said earlier, this in no way suggests that Cornelius did not need to hear the gospel of Christ. It was precisely because Cornelius and his family were recipients of God's prior work of grace that the Lord was so eager to send his Apostle to them to explain faith's proper content—the life, teaching, death and resurrection of Jesus, not to mention the gift of the Holy Spirit.[35]

The same point can probably be seen in the Lord's enigmatic statement to Paul in Acts 18 (again in a vision) at the beginning of the Corinthian mission. Jesus encourages Paul to stay in Corinth despite persecution because "there are many in this city who are my people" (Acts 18:10, NRSV). Who are these 'many' people of God? The simplest explanation is that Corinth contained numerous men and women of true faith, just like Cornelius, who upon hearing Paul's gospel will respond rightly and join God's visible people. According to Acts, this is a reason to continue preaching in Corinth, not to leave the city and go somewhere else.

Pessimism and hope

The question of what happens to those who have never heard the gospel is a very difficult one. It deserves more attention than we have given it. Nevertheless, we hope that we have offered a satisfying outline of what we can and cannot know from the Scriptures—the only reliable judge of our thoughts.

The basic stance of the Bible toward those outside God's visible family is one of utter pessimism. All men and women deserve judgment for their failure to heed the universal obligation to revere the Creator and care for their neighbours. When God's wrath is revealed, no-one will be able to say they did not know what the Creator expected of them. This fact should inspire godly sorrow as well as prayer and zeal to promote the gospel in whatever way we can. For Christ's atoning death and resurrection is the only means of mercy, and faith in him is the only assurance of salvation.

Nevertheless, in tension with this biblical pessimism is a restrained hope grounded in equally biblical ideas. God is at perfect liberty to have mercy on whomever he wishes. What has been revealed to us in the gospel is to be believed and obeyed and proclaimed but it always remains true that "the secret things belong to the Lord our God" (Deut 29:29). God is the Lord of all creation and he is free to act in the world however he wishes. It would be a mistake to affirm categorically that God will save *no-one* outside his visible people.

Will God accept some of those who have never heard the gospel? We don't know. What we do know is that the Lord is absolutely free to do so (because of Jesus' death and resurrection) and that on at least two occasions in Scripture he appears to have done just that (Melchizedek, Cornelius' family). Because of this, we believe it is legitimate and healthy for Christians, amid their profound pessimism about humanity and tireless zeal for mission, to hold a glimmer of hope that God will extend his mercy beyond the historical and geographical reach of the church's proclamation.

10 | Life after life-after-death

The myth about life-after-death

WE ARRIVE NOW AT one of the most undervalued and sometimes misunderstood aspects of the Bible's description of the future: the topic of life-after-death or, more accurately, as we will see, life *after* life-after-death.

What happens beyond death is one of those areas—like the idea of a Rapture prior to a Second Coming—where myths have crept into popular Christian thought which have little connection either with the Bible or with what the historic church has taught throughout the centuries. So, we will state the myth and then the doctrine we are going to explore below.

> *The modern myth.* When Christians die, their bodies decay once and for all while their spirits go eternally to God's presence in heaven.

> *The biblical doctrine.* When Christians die, they rest temporarily in God's presence in heaven until they are bodily raised to life to enjoy forever God's new creation.

We will unpack the 'new creation' part of this statement in Chapters 12–13, when we come to grips with the fact that the Bible envisages God's eternal kingdom as a new earth in which

God himself—just as in the Garden of Eden—will dwell with humanity.

In this chapter we want to talk about the first part of the above summary statement. The Bible and the historic Christian church has usually taught that 'eternal life' is not a disembodied spirit-life but a gloriously resurrected *bodily* life.

Resurrection in the Apostles' Creed

The point is stated perfectly in the famous Apostles' Creed which has been a standard summary of Christian belief since its origins in the third century. It is affirmed by both Roman Catholic and Protestant churches. There are two references in this creed to the 'afterlife'. One relates to Jesus, and the other to Christians in general. Both concern the essential idea of bodily resurrection:

I believe in God, the Father almighty,
creator of heaven and earth.
I believe in Jesus Christ, God's only Son, our Lord,
who was conceived by the Holy Spirit,
born of the Virgin Mary,
suffered under Pontius Pilate,
was crucified, died, and was buried;
he descended to the dead.
On the third day he rose again;
he ascended into heaven,
he is seated at the right hand of the Father,
and he will come again to judge the living and the dead.
I believe in the Holy Spirit,
the holy catholic church,
the communion of saints,

the forgiveness of sins,
the resurrection of the body,
and the life everlasting. AMEN.

Sometimes even long-term church goers assume that the reference at the end of the creed to "the resurrection of the body and the life everlasting" reiterates what is said earlier about Jesus' resurrection ("on the third day he rose again"). However, it is quite clear that the final five lines are all about believers, not Jesus. Following the teaching of the New Testament, the Apostles' Creed states that just as "on the third day (Jesus) rose again", so at the end of history men and women will experience their own "resurrection of the body", and it is in this *bodily* mode that we will enjoy "the life everlasting." Historically, in other words, the Christian view of the afterlife has always envisaged resurrected bodies in a revived creation not immortal spirits in an eternal heaven. That is what the Kingdom of God is all about—the Lord's reign over all creation.

This, we hope, comes as a great relief to some readers, since some of the most *unattractive* images of our future life involve strange, Casper-the-ghost humanoids floating about in a bright blue sky full of glowing clouds. Such erroneous visions of the human future have damaged our enthusiasm for God's plans!

Resurrection in the Old Testament

Before we look at the New Testament teaching on this theme, we want to wind the clock back several centuries and point out that the "resurrection of the body" was a peculiarly *Jewish* belief in the ancient world.

Pictures of the afterlife in Egyptian, Roman and Greek culture were, in principle, *bodiless*. The souls of the departed were thought to leave the physical realm and enter a sometimes hopeful, often gloomy, netherworld of gods and spirits. Interestingly, the early Old Testament writers sometimes suggest a similarly pessimistic view of the afterlife. There is the occasional hint of consciousness after death (e.g. Gen 5:24; 1 Sam 28:7–19) but, mostly, death is described as a shadowy and unknown end. For example:

> JOB 7:9–10. As a cloud vanishes and is gone, so he who goes
> down to the grave does not return. He will never come to
> his house again; his place will know him no more.

> PSALM 6:4–5. Turn, O LORD, and deliver me; save me
> because of your unfailing love. No-one remembers you
> when he is dead. Who praises you from his grave?

But things are a little different in the later Old Testament writings. Here the beautiful Jewish doctrine of God as Creator and Sustainer of physical life is rightly applied to beliefs about the afterlife. How could the God who lovingly fashioned the physical world and called it all "very good" (Gen 1:31) possibly intend to discard physicality and replace it with a ghostly netherworld? *No!* said these biblical writers inspired by God's Spirit, the Creator will not abandon his creation. He will revive it.

Enter: the wonderful Jewish doctrine of the resurrection of the dead. One of the first hints of resurrection life for God's people comes in a vision of Ezekiel, where the prophet sees a valley full of dry bones which we are told represents the destroyed nation of Israel. He is told to speak to the bones God's words of life:

> EZEKIEL 37:4–6. 'Dry bones, hear the word of the LORD!
> This is what the Sovereign LORD says to these bones : I will
> make breath enter you, and you will come to life. I will
> attach tendons to you and make flesh come upon you and

cover you with skin; I will put breath in you, and you will come to life. Then you will know that I am the LORD.'

The bones obey and the people of Israel come back to life (Ezek 37:7–10). Admittedly, it is far from clear whether the resurrection spoken of in this prophetic vision is metaphorical or concrete. At points the description appears literal, at other times symbolic.

The book of Daniel takes this resurrection theme and applies it to the concrete fate of the departed:

> DANIEL 12:1–4. But at that time your people—everyone whose name is found written in the book—will be delivered. Multitudes who sleep in the dust of the earth will awake: some to everlasting life, others to shame and everlasting contempt. Those who are wise will shine like the brightness of the heavens, and those who lead many to righteousness, like the stars for ever and ever. But you, Daniel, close up and seal the words of the scroll until the time of the end.

This passage establishes forever the Jewish doctrine of the resurrection of the dead at the "time of the end", a theme that appears throughout ancient Jewish literature: in the Dead Sea Scrolls, Josephus, the Pseudepigrapha, the Mishnah, the Talmud and other writings.

Jesus and the resurrection

Not surprisingly, the first Christians inherited this Old Testament doctrine of a 'General Resurrection'. They did so with one unexpected addition. They insisted that a specific resurrection had already taken place *ahead of time*. The Messiah himself had experienced the end-time resurrection within history in April AD 30. This was quite an addition, and we need to consider its significance further.

For now it is worth making clear just how pervasive in the New Testament is this belief in a General Resurrection at the end of time. Jesus, of course, taught it. In answer to the Sadducees, a Jewish sect which denied the resurrection, he said:

> MATTHEW 22:29–33. Jesus answered them, "You are wrong, because you know neither the scriptures nor the power of God. For in the resurrection they neither marry nor are given in marriage, but are like angels in heaven. And as for the resurrection of the dead, have you not read what was said to you by God, 'I am the God of Abraham, the God of Isaac, and the God of Jacob'? He is God not of the dead, but of the living." And when the crowd heard it, they were astounded at his teaching.

And,

> LUKE 14:13–14. But when you give a banquet, invite the poor, the crippled, the lame, the blind, and you will be blessed. Although they cannot repay you, you will be repaid at the resurrection of the righteous.

And, once more:

> JOHN 5:28–29. Do not be astonished at this; for the hour is coming when all who are in their graves will hear his voice and will come out—those who have done good, to the resurrection of life, and those who have done evil, to the resurrection of condemnation.

It is the Apostle Paul, however, writing well after April AD 30, who is able to explain how this General Resurrection taught by

Jesus (and the Old Testament) relates to the specific resurrection of the Messiah himself.

Paul on the resurrection

In 1 Corinthians 15 Paul offers his most detailed treatment of the General Resurrection. From the way he argues it seems that some in the church of Corinth had trouble coming to grips with the idea of the dead being raised at the end of time. They accepted Jesus' resurrection—they were Christians, after all; they just weren't so sure about the General Resurrection. Being Greeks many of them would have been raised to think of the afterlife as a netherworld of gods and spirits. According to Greek thinking, the body is something you escape at death.

Paul responds to these pagan assumptions the way he so often responds to errors of thinking: by brilliantly tying his fine Jewish theology to the historical realities of Jesus. In other words, he links the teaching of the Old Testament with the gospel of Jesus' death and resurrection. In particular, he explains the connection between Jesus' resurrection and the ancient biblical doctrine of a General Resurrection. The General Resurrection, Paul says, has been pre-empted, and therefore initiated, by the resurrection of the Messiah:

> 1 CORINTHIANS 15:20–23. But Christ has indeed been raised from the dead, the firstfruits of those who have fallen asleep. For since death came through a man, the resurrection of the dead comes also through a man. For as in Adam all die, so in Christ all will be made alive. But each in his own turn: Christ, the firstfruits; then, when he comes, those who belong to him.

Paul describes the risen Jesus as the 'firstfruits'. This is an agricultural term for the *initial produce* of a coming harvest. In this context it means that Jesus is the first indication—the inauguration—of God's great future harvest when he revives the dead and renews the creation. In Jesus' resurrection God has demonstrated within historical time what the Old Testament promised he would do at the "time of the end" (Dan 12:4).

As the firstfruits Jesus is also a kind of 'Adam' figure: "For as in Adam all die, so in Christ all will be made alive" (verse 22). Again, the Apostle is operating in a thoroughly Old Testament frame of mind. According to the opening chapters of Genesis, the entire history of humanity could be observed in the story of the first human being. Adam was fashioned by the loving hands of the Creator only to turn his back on the Almighty. He preferred autonomy instead of a relationship with the Creator. By defying his Creator, Adam launched sin and death.[36]

What Adam was to this earthly kingdom, Jesus is to God's future kingdom: the progenitor and paradigm of a new humanity. Jesus is the original of the species, as it were, and he shapes our destiny.

And that destiny is resurrection life. Verse 22 again: "For as in Adam all die, so in Christ all will be made alive. But each in his own turn: Christ, the firstfruits; then, when he comes, those who belong to him." Christ's resurrection, in other words, is God's guarantee—his down-payment—of what he has promised to do for all: the renewal of bodily life.

Naturally, this raises all sorts of questions, not the least of which is: what kind of body will we have in the resurrection? Paul pre-empts that question a little later in the chapter:

1 Corinthians 15:35–44. But someone may ask, "How are the dead raised? With what kind of body will they come?" How foolish! What you sow does not come to life unless it dies. When you sow, you do not plant the body that will be, but just a seed, perhaps of wheat or of something else … So will it be with the resurrection of the dead. The body that is sown is perishable, it is raised imperishable; it is sown in dishonour, it is raised in glory; it is sown in weakness, it is raised in power; it is sown a natural body, it is raised a spiritual body.

Whatever you do, please don't see the word 'spiritual' there in verse 44 and think Paul is talking about 'bodilessness'. This has nothing to do with the old mythical view of our souls floating disembodied in the presence of God. Paul—in fact, the whole Bible—is adamant that whatever changes will occur at the resurrection, we will still have a 'body'. It will be a 'spiritual' body, Paul says, as opposed to a merely 'natural' (or in Greek, *soulish*) body.

So, what on earth (or heaven) is a 'spiritual body'? Paul just means that the resurrection body will be one fully endowed with God's life-giving Spirit. This idea is connected to the strong biblical promise, explored in Chapter 1, that the coming kingdom of God will be a world saturated by God's Spirit (Ezek 37:11–14; Joel 2:28–29).[37] Paul is not referring to a ghostly spirit but to a body ignited by the Spirit of God.[38]

This bodily aspect of Christian hope is so much a part of New Testament thought that Paul later in Romans 8 can even define our salvation as the 'redemption of our bodies' (when was the last time you thought of salvation in these terms?):

Romans 8:22–24. We know that the whole creation has been groaning as in the pains of childbirth right up to the present time. Not only so, but we ourselves, who have the

firstfruits of the Spirit [i.e. the down-payment of the full
endowment of the Spirit in God's kingdom], groan inwardly
as we wait eagerly for our adoption as sons, the *redemption
of our bodies*. For in this hope we were saved.

At the centre of Christian hope is the redemption not just of
our spirits or souls but of our *bodies*. Eternal life involves a
Spirit-endowed bodily resurrection guaranteed by and modelled
on Jesus' own resurrection.[39]

The intermediate state: what happens before the resurrection?

All of this raises an obvious question: what happens in between
death now and resurrection in God's kingdom? It might
surprise you to learn that the Bible says very little about that
question—so great is its emphasis on the General Resurrection
as the defining reality of our hope beyond the grave.

It is because of this that numerous theologians and Bible
teachers over the centuries have taught a doctrine known as
soul-sleep. According to this theory, those who die with faith in
Christ 'sleep' *unconscious* in the protective care of God until the
day of resurrection. This might sound strange to many but
proponents of this view are just trying to do justice to the
frequent New Testament insistence that eternal life is
resurrection life and that the period in between death and
resurrection is to be thought of as a kind of 'sleep' (Acts 13:36;
1 Cor 11:30, 15:51; 1 Thess 4:15; 2 Peter 3:4).

It has to be said, however, that soul-sleep is not the majority
view. Most theologians (whether Protestant or Roman Catholic)
insist that in between death and the day of resurrection departed

believers are *consciously* at rest—as spirits—in the presence of God in heaven. This is known in theology as the 'doctrine of the intermediate state'. Below we will explore the usual biblical arguments for an intermediate state but it is perhaps worth pointing out at this stage that we, the authors, differ slightly from each other on this question. One of us prefers to emphasise the 'sleeping' nature of the afterlife (before resurrection) and the other is happy to think of the faithful departed as *conscious* in God's care.

The idea of a conscious intermediate state following death is hinted at in at least three passages. The first is Luke 23, where Jesus makes that famous promise to the criminal crucified next to him:

> LUKE 23:42–43. Then he said, "Jesus, remember me when you come into your kingdom." Jesus answered him, "I tell you the truth, today you will be with me in paradise."

You could argue that the word 'today' refers to the resurrection day, since, on the soul-sleep view, the next thing the criminal would know would be rising to life in God's kingdom. But for many readers of the New Testament this does not seem the natural sense of the words. More probable, they say, is that Jesus really is promising 'paradise' for the man at the moment of his death prior to resurrection. Of course, this could just be a metaphorical expression of a beautiful sleep in God's presence, but the term 'paradise' (in Greek as well as in English) does suggest a place which is *experienced* as bliss.[40]

The second passage is from Paul who explains to the Philippians that, viewed from one angle, death is preferable to life because it means being with Jesus:

PHILIPPIANS 1:21–24. For to me, to live is Christ and to die is gain. If I am to go on living in the body, this will mean fruitful labour for me. Yet what shall I choose? I do not know! I am torn between the two: I desire to depart and be with Christ, which is better by far; but it is more necessary for you that I remain in the body.

A similar preference for death over life, perhaps suggesting an intermediate state, appears in 2 Corinthians:

2 CORINTHIANS 4:7–9. We live by faith, not by sight. We are confident, I say, and would prefer to be away from the body and at home with the Lord. So we make it our goal to please him, whether we are at home in the body or away from it.

Again, one could interpret these passages to mean that following death the next thing we will know is resurrection life 'at home with the Lord' in God's kingdom. Paul would then be looking forward to the rest that comes from leaving this life behind and being safe with his Lord. But this is not an obvious interpretation for many theologians. It really does seem as though Paul is teaching that in between death and resurrection believers are 'with Christ' in a state that is preferable to life here and now. It is not yet the glorious resurrection life but it is a good experience, which suggests to most that those who 'sleep' in Christ are aware of the fact. Perhaps they are enjoying the most realistic dream of their life.

There is a fourth passage that is sometimes thought to indicate consciousness in between death and resurrection. It is Jesus' famous parable of the Rich Man and Lazarus (Luke 16:19–31). In the parable a rich man neglects the poverty and suffering of a man called Lazarus. The rich man then dies and goes to *hadēs*, the place of the dead. Lazarus also dies and goes to 'Abraham's side' in heaven. A conversation then breaks out between the rich man, who is in torment because of his neglect of the poor, and Abraham:

> LUKE 16:19–31. There was a rich man who was dressed in purple and fine linen and who feasted sumptuously every day. And at his gate lay a poor man named Lazarus, covered with sores, who longed to satisfy his hunger with what fell from the rich man's table; even the dogs would come and lick his sores. The poor man died and was carried away by the angels to be with Abraham. The rich man also died and was buried. In Hades, where he was being tormented, he looked up and saw Abraham far away with Lazarus by his side. He called out, 'Father Abraham, have mercy on me, and send Lazarus to dip the tip of his finger in water and cool my tongue; for I am in agony in these flames.' But Abraham said, 'Child, remember that during your lifetime you received your good things, and Lazarus in like manner evil things; but now he is comforted here, and you are in agony. Besides all this, between you and us a great chasm has been fixed, so that those who might want to pass from here to you cannot do so, and no-one can cross from there to us.' He said, 'Then, father, I beg you to send him to my father's house—for I have five brothers—that he may warn them, so that they will not also come into this place of torment.' Abraham replied, 'They have Moses and the prophets; they should listen to them.' He said, 'No, father Abraham; but if someone goes to them from the dead, they will repent.' He said to him, 'If they do not listen to Moses and the prophets, neither will they be convinced even if someone rises from the dead.'

The obvious punch-line of the parable is that once you are dead there is no crossing over from one side to the other. The one who rejects the path of godly compassion in this life—whose faith does not express itself in love (Gal 5:6)—will be separated forever from the abode of the faithful. In passing we should note the similarities between this parable and the parable of the Sheep and the Goats (Matt 25:31–46) where neglect of the needy is likewise portrayed as a reason for eternal punishment.

But what does the parable tell us specifically about the afterlife? Probably not much. The problem with getting any afterlife theology out of this story is that it is a parable. It is an entirely imaginative scenario designed to drive home the very urgent message that men and women must decide now before it is too late. Taking the parable literally, as a concrete account of life after death, would lead to all sorts of absurdities, not the least of which is the suggestion that in the hereafter the unsaved and the saved are within *cooee* of each other.

It is probably even too much to conclude from Luke 16:19–31 that those who die outside of Christ are *conscious* in torment (before being resurrected and condemned to *Gehenna*). The text is sometimes thought to suggest this but, as we have just said, a parable is not a good place from which to extract such a significant theological idea.

Leaving this parable to one side, all we can say with confidence about the doctrine of the intermediate state is that those who die *in Christ's mercy* rest in some satisfying way in paradise at home with the Lord (we know even less about what happens to unbelievers prior to the Judgment).

That is, *until* their resurrection.

The 'intermediate state' is exactly what the terminology suggests: it is a temporary arrangement until all the dead are raised for judgment. Those who are outside of Christ will be condemned justly and in proportion to their deeds. Those who are *in* Christ will be saved from condemnation because of Jesus' death and will enjoy a transformed bodily existence guaranteed by and modeled on Christ's own resurrection life. Put simply, eternal life in the Bible is the Resurrection Life that follows what we normally think of as life-after-death.

A s we write this book, the turn of the millennium has faded from general consciousness. But for a while there in the 1990s, every second book or article had "The End of…" in its title. The 'pressure' of the calendar clicking over to the Year 2000 brought with it all sorts of anxieties and expectations. The Y2K bug was big business, as computer geeks earned obscene amounts of money trying to make sure that computers wouldn't meltdown when the clock struck midnight on December 31, 1999. Theories were developed about the end of the age, with the accompanying murmur that we could be on the eve of some terrible change.

Human beings seem to be wired towards having a 'sense of an ending'. We seem to need the feeling that something is about to end, a new thing is about to begin, events are coming to a head and then some sort of climactic event will take place. Perhaps it is part of the way we give meaning to our lives, a shape to our every day existence and a place within the greater scheme of things.

Whatever the psychological reasons for the human sense of an ending, is it a notion found in the Bible?

We have already explored the biblical understanding of death and judgment for individuals and creation, but the question of the world's end has a special fascination. It's an idea that attracts singers and poets. "It's the end of the world as we know it, and I feel fine", sang REM's Michael Stipe. Those whose musical tastes were formed in the 60s and 70s will recall Barry McGuire singing, "Ah, you don't believe, we're on the eve of destruction". In a different mood, the poet T S Eliot wrote: "This is the way the world ends, not with a bang but a whimper".

But when we turn to the Bible, does it teach an end of the world?

The answer is not straightforward, though on reflection it leans towards a clear 'no'. This may come as a shock to many readers, who have (like us) been brought up on a diet of apocalypse and rapture. Just as with Rapture theology we saw that a lot of speculation came out of little scriptural data, so with the apocalypse (for that is the commonly used word for talking about the end of the world, even though it is actually the Greek word for 'revelation') Bible readers have extrapolated an elaborate potential cosmic history from a range of otherwise-intentioned Bible passages.

We can summarise the Bible's teachings under four headings:

(1) Prophecies about the destruction of nations

There are many Old Testament prophecies in which the Lord condemns the nations for oppressing the people of Israel, and condemns Israel for forgetting the ways of their God. In these prophecies, strong universal language is often used. Here is an example:

> JEREMIAH 51:29. The land trembles and writhes, for the Lord's purposes against Babylon stand—to lay waste the land of Babylon so that no-one will live there.

To most readers, this is obviously a prophecy about specific places, and specific events around them. However, some Bible interpreters use Old Testament prophecies such as this to make outrageous statements about world events today and their importance for the supposed coming apocalypse.

Take, for example, our verse from Jeremiah 51. Look up any Bible dictionary or standard commentary and you will find that scholars are discussing the relationship between Babylon and Israel in the sixth century BC. Their concerns will be historical. However, to illustrate our point, at least one modern-day pastor writes this about Jeremiah 51:29:

> Iraq is the modern name for the ancient land of Babylon … It is a land long associated with rebellion against God. It is the area in which the Garden of Eden, the seat of rebellion, was located. It will be the seat of rebellion at the end of this age. Its ancient capital, Babylon, will feature once more in opposition to God and His people.
>
> The chapter we have before us, coupled with Revelation 18, presents to us the judgment that God has planned for that city and its rebellion. What is happening there at present does serve as a foreshadowing of future events.[41]

This kind of biblical speculation is entirely wrongheaded. There is no good reason to think of this Bible prophecy as probable code for an apocalypse-heralding event that we can identify with the current war in Iraq!

The many Old Testament prophecies against the nations are just that—declarations of judgment on those nations (coupled with pleas to Israel to repent of its own wickedness).

(2) Large-scale or cosmic apocalypses

In some parts of the Bible, God's judgment is described in language that is frighteningly cosmic and overwhelming. One such chapter is Isaiah 24, which comes after a series of prophecies against the nations of the earth who have opposed Yahweh and his people. In Chapter 24, this 'operatic' judgment reaches its peak in a prophecy of even greater destruction:

> ISAIAH 24:1–23. See, the LORD is going to lay waste the earth and devastate it; he will ruin its face and scatter its inhabitants— [2] it will be the same for priest as for people, for master as for servant, for mistress as for maid, for seller as for buyer, for borrower as for lender, for debtor as for creditor. [3] The earth will be completely laid waste and totally plundered. The LORD has spoken this word. [4] The earth dries up and withers, the world languishes and withers …
>
> [23] The moon will be abashed, the sun ashamed; for the LORD Almighty will reign on Mount Zion and in Jerusalem, and before its elders, gloriously.

You get the picture …

Surely this passage is describing a cosmic disaster—an end to the world—isn't it? The Lord will devastate the whole earth such that it is *completely* laid waste, dries up and withers. It is hard to imagine a more complete destruction. But even in this passage of ultimate judgment, there is a sense that this is not the end of the road for planet earth. Its inhabitants are scattered, ruined and distressed—but not all destroyed. The earth is split, shaken and falls—and yet, verse 23 adds that "the LORD Almighty will reign on Mount Zion and in Jerusalem", which certainly sounds like it's on earth.

Clearly, this passage is not describing the obliteration of the earth, but its condemnation. In fact, it is not the earth that is being judged, but the people who have defiled it (verse 5). They must bear the guilt for the curse on the earth; it's their fault that the devastation is coming.[42]

The cosmic apocalypse is rare in the Old Testament, but we haven't yet mentioned its source. The original apocalypse is the flood recounted in Genesis 6–8, which destroys every living thing except what was in the ark. The flood story is the background to biblical teaching about the end of the world, and this is all the more important because it ends with one of God's great promises:

> GENESIS 9:11. I establish my covenant with you: Never again will all life be cut off by the waters of a flood; never again will there be a flood to destroy the earth.

The Noah story is mentioned in the one New Testament passage that at first read seems to suggest an apocalyptic scenario for the world. In 2 Peter 3, the Apostle draws a parallel between the waters of the flood and the fires of judgment day:

> 2 PETER 3:6–7. By these waters also the world of that time was deluged and destroyed. By the same word the present heavens and earth are reserved for fire, being kept for the day of judgment and destruction of ungodly men.

Notice that the emphasis is on condemning "ungodly men" not removing the physical world itself (the flood, of course, did not obliterate planet earth). This passage is arguably one of the most apocalyptic of the whole Bible, and we will return to it in the next chapter.

It may surprise readers to discover that the earth is not destroyed in the book of Revelation, the book that we usually turn to for our apocalyptic scenarios. Death and Hades are destroyed in the lake of fire of Revelation 20—but the earth is not. Rather, the first earth simply passes into the second earth without an apocalypse on view!

(3) Armageddon

Perhaps the most apocalyptic idea in all Christian thinking is the battle of Armageddon. In some kinds of eschatology, usually varieties of premillennialism, enormous attention is given to the idea that at the end of the world there will be an intense battle between the armies of heaven and the kings of the earth, which will end in the earth's devastation. Using the technique of Bible reading that we have been questioning throughout this book—finding past or future historical parallels with Bible passages that were never meant to be read that way—Christian teachers with this eschatology urge upon their congregations that there will be this almighty battle before the final judgment.

The Bible passages used to support this approach are Zechariah 14, Ezekiel 38–39 and Revelation 16–20—though we should point out, the word 'Armageddon' itself occurs just once in the Bible (Rev 16:16). In these passages, God fights for his people against Israel's oppressors or (in Revelation) against the dragon, Satan. This is taught to be the final clash between God's forces of good and Satan's soldiers of evil.

The name for this battle is Armageddon because it is believed it will take place at Mount Megiddo, where other famous battles have been held (e.g. 2 Kings 23:29–30). Having said that, we have counted at least ten different scholarly views on the meaning of Armageddon.[43]

Armageddon is sometimes lifted out of the geography books and into the action comics genre, as people ingeniously but foolishly try to work out which earthly forces will fight the Lord in the final battle. The most famous identification of the battlers was by Hal Lindsey in *The Late Great Planet Earth*, who claimed that God's forces would be the Western nations while the devil's charges would be 200 million Chinese! You could probably guess that in the *Left Behind* series mentioned in an earlier chapter, *Armageddon* (Book 11) places the battle in the Middle East.

Our objections to this kind of Bible reading have been raised many times. It misunderstands the kind of biblical literature in which these battles are discussed. They simply aren't blueprints for the history of world wars; they ought not be used for racist and nationalist judgments about who is on the Lord's side; and they do not fit with the broader biblical picture of the end of the world.

The quest for Armageddon is one of the great follies of the church. If there is a final battle on earth, it will not need our encouragement or speculation in order to achieve God's purposes.

(4) The world that is passing away

Another type of biblical writing about the end of the world is less violent and judgmental. A number of New Testament texts speak of this world passing away and a new one beginning. In contrast with the image of conflagration in 2 Peter 3, or the prophecies of destruction, these metaphors are more passive. In one of his sayings that is repeated in a number of Gospels, Jesus says that "Heaven and earth will pass away, but my words will never pass away" (Matt 24:35; Mark 13:31; Luke 21:33). Similarly, he says that nothing of the Law will disappear until "heaven and earth disappear" (Matt 5:18; Luke 16:17). These are rhetorical flourishes from Jesus, but they suggest that he understood that this world comes to an end in some sense.

1 Corinthians 7:31 teaches that this world in its present form is passing away (as does 1 John 2:17). Not everything about our way of life will have much value in the coming Kingdom. This passage suggests we should sit lightly to the concerns of this world—our emotions, our belongings, our occupations. For we will pass into the next age, and we ought to start living with its values now. Other letters highlight that we are to live not according to the principles of this world, but those of the world to come (Gal 6:14; Col 2:8, 20).

Eventually, in Revelation 21, we reach that great moment when the new has come and the old is entirely gone. But this is not a moment of obliteration in Revelation; it is one of transformation, of the passing away of the old to reveal the new.

> REVELATION 21:1, 4. Then I saw a new heaven and a new earth, for the first heaven and the first earth had *passed away*, and there was no longer any sea…There will be no more death or mourning or crying or pain, for the old order of things has *passed away*.

In summary, there has been an unhelpful over-emphasis on the apocalyptic pictures of the world's future. When we consider the way the Bible talks about the end of the world, we have to conclude that it is not apparent there will be a great day of obliteration, as it is sometimes imagined. A day of judgment remains for human beings but the future of the earth itself is one of renewal and rightness.

Future scenarios

If we have established that the Bible doesn't teach that the world will end, is there anything we can know about what will happen between now and the day of judgment?

In fact, there are a number of things we can know, not from the Bible this time, but from science. Science teaches that this world, earth, will end—and end badly. Scientists are as certain as they can be that in around 5 billion years, the sun will expand and burn earth to a frazzle. The universe will either expand endlessly, with the world growing colder and duller, or contract (they call it 'the big crunch'). Although the timescale of this seems unfathomable to us, the trajectory is very clear: the universe is headed for futility. These discoveries led the renowned atheist physicist, Stephen Weinberg, to remark, "The more the universe seems comprehensible, the more it also seems pointless".

We can add to this gloomy long-term prognosis the gloomy short-term prognosis that the climate change scientists are currently developing. The science of climate change is still young, but a consistent picture is emerging that we human beings have heated up the earth's atmosphere to detrimental effect, and it may even be too late to do much about it. And nuclear warfare still remains a large threat, especially with political tensions between countries such as the USA and Iran or North Korea—how long until someone loses their nerve and 'presses the button'?

All of these scenarios suggest that we human beings could do a decent job of destroying the world ourselves.

The Christian hope rests on the arrival (the *parousia*) of the Lord Jesus Christ. Our hope is that God will intervene in these terrible trajectories of our planet. And the Bible gives us reason to hope that his intervention will bring a new heaven and new earth, forged and refashioned out of the current one, by the power of the Creator who can make all things new.

We need not fear an end of this world that is out of our control (even though it is), because it is not out of God's control. The power of the risen Lord Jesus will prevail over all apocalyptic anxieties and follies.

In *The Hitchhiker's Guide to the Galaxy*, the earth was blown up unceremoniously by visiting aliens to make way for an interplanetary bypass. All-powerful though he is, Yahweh, the God of Israel, the Father of our Lord Jesus Christ has *no* such intentions. He does not plan to destroy the earth. The earth is his, along with everything in it. He promised way back in the days of Noah never to destroy it in righteous anger again. The Bible confirms that God will judge the earth, not that he will obliterate it.

Our God has other plans for planet earth.

12 | The future genesis

A world of contradictions

ALL OF US HAVE HAD moments in life when the sheer beauty and order of the world are undeniable. John's most recent experience came on the last family holiday, when sitting on Coolum Beach, eating dinner as the sun went down on a gorgeous day. The waves were washing peacefully against the shore, the meal was delicious, and he and his wife Buff snuggled as they watched the kids playing together *happily*. They could have sat there for hours.

Greg and his family caught a flash of glory on a recent afternoon walk past an aquarium. Popping their heads through a window, they were overwhelmed by shocks of colour and light as myriads of delightful and amazing tropical fish flashed back and forth across the tank. Unbelievable creatures—fish you thought only existed in stories; cube fish, tubes with frondlike tails, paper-thin fish that disappear completely when you see them head on. The sense of wonder brought a thrill to them all and they stood there gawping until the owner had to ask them to leave.

In moments like these it is easy to conclude that planet earth is a place of unhindered beauty. And in a sense that is right.

But it only takes the flick of a remote control—or, for most of us eventually, first-hand experience—to discover that all is not well. This 'beautiful place' has a habit of turning ugly. It dishes out tsunamis, droughts, miscarriages, ozone holes, cancers, and the list goes on. It suddenly becomes easy to think of planet earth as a place of cruelty or, at least, of what atheist Professor Richard Dawkins describes as "nothing but blind, pitiless indifference".[44]

And in a sense that is right, too.

There is, in other words, what appears to be an unresolvable tension, even contradiction, in our world, between its undeniable beauty and its manifest ugliness.

The shape of hope: the eschatology of Genesis 1–2

From its opening chapters, the Bible is upfront about this contradiction. Genesis 1 and 2 describe in idyllic terms the beauty and goodness of the created order. The refrain "and it was good" occurs seven times in Chapter 1 alone. And Genesis 2:10–23 goes on to describe that "good" in terms of harmony in the social, spiritual and physical spheres of life.

But when we turn the page to Genesis 3 suddenly we are confronted with the not-so-good. The social relationship between the Man and the Woman breaks down; the spiritual connection between human beings and God collapses; and the physical environment itself becomes corrupted, crystallised in the ominous words to Adam:

> GENESIS 3:17–19. Cursed is the ground because of you; through painful toil you will eat of it all the days of your life. [18] It will produce thorns and thistles for you, and you will eat the plants of the field. [19] By the sweat of your brow you will eat your food until you return to the ground, since from it you were taken; for dust you are and to dust you will return.

The words, "Cursed is the ground because of you; through painful toil you will eat of it all the days of your life", signal the end of harmony in the physical sphere. No longer will Adam's work in the garden be marked only by fruitfulness and joy. Now 'thorns and thistles' will spoil the environmental bliss. Eden is lost, henceforth only to be glimpsed in the fleeting beauties of an imperfect world.

But, of course, this is not the end, and Genesis never was meant to be read that way. The tragic narrative at the front of the Bible is not there simply as a lament, decrying how bad things have become. Nor is it just what anthropologists call an 'aetiology', a narrative explanation of why things are the way they are (as many Aboriginal Dreamtime stories function).

Genesis 1 and 2 are also about *eschatology*, about the way things *will be* when the Creator fulfils his purposes. The contrast between the Ideal of Genesis 1 and 2 and the Fall of Genesis 3 is as much a contrast between God's ultimate intentions for the world and our current experience of it. Put another way, the picture of Genesis 1 and 2 is, in part, intended to provide *hope* for those living in the shadow of Genesis 3: hope that God the Creator will restore the Ideal. The very fact that an angel with a fiery sword blocks the passage back into Eden (Gen 3:24) begs the question: How will they get back in? How will this calamity be reversed? Knowing the Ideal is there, but out of reach, pushes us to hope for a return.

Perhaps an analogy will help. Imagine a child born with a disability that could only be treated once he turned five. Until that day he knew only the frailties and restrictions of his condition. The day comes for him to meet the specialist in charge of his case, who begins not by explaining the condition itself or the treatment to follow but by describing how a healthy child's body is meant to work. As the doctor paints a picture of the ideal, the young boy's mind is filled with thoughts about the possibilities—the running, the climbing, the rumbling. Even as they move on to discuss the condition and the treatment, the boy cannot get out of his head the doctor's wonderful picture of perfect health. And it is this image of perfection, happiness and fulfilment that will sustain him in the difficult months ahead. It will give him hope.

This, we believe, is how we are meant to approach the opening pages of the Bible. Genesis 1 and 2 provide us with a picture of health to which the creation will ultimately be restored. It is eschatology as well as aetiology. It's a vision of what shall be as well as a description of what was.

Please be clear, we are not denying that the narrative of Genesis 1 and 2 was also written to emphasise God's original fashioning of the world (and a real historical Fall in Gen 3). However, we are trying to make an additional point that is sometimes overlooked. It is precisely because the Creator *is* as he is described in these texts—powerful, ordered and devoted to his creation—that we are to read Genesis not simply as a picture of the past but also, and especially, as a promise about the future. Genesis 1 and 2, in other words, establish the basis and shape of our future hope. Let us unpack this a little more.

We explained in Chapter 10 that the Bible's doctrine of the afterlife as the resurrection of the body owed everything to the wonderful Jewish doctrine of God as the Creator of physical life. How could the God who lovingly fashioned creation and called it all "very good" (Gen 1:31) possibly intend ultimately to discard physicality and replace it with a ghostly netherworld! No, said the Old Testament writers under the inspiration of God's Spirit, the

Creator will not abandon his creation. He will revive it. Eternal life, therefore, cannot be a disembodied ghostly life modelled on ancient pagan thought. It involves, rather, a bodily resurrected life premised on the doctrine of God as Creator and, of course, guaranteed by the reality of Christ's resurrection.

A similar logic lies behind the Bible's promise about God's eternal kingdom, the home of our bodily resurrected life. Pagan notions of a soul*ish* netherworld are nowhere to be found. What we see instead is a single-minded affirmation that the Ideal of creation established in Genesis 1 and 2 is the foundation of the Bible's teaching about God's promised future. When the Bible writers dare to describe the Coming Kingdom, they never reach for the imagery of spirits, harps and halos; they grab hold of Genesis 1 and 2 and say two words: new creation.

New creation in Isaiah 65

Take the greatest of Israel's prophets, Isaiah, writing 700 years before Christ during one of the lowest points in biblical history, a period when the contradictions of life this side of Genesis 3 were being felt acutely. The prophet declares that out of the ruins of Israel, indeed of the entire condemned world, God will prove faithful not only to his creatures but also to his creation. This beautiful passage deserves to be quoted in full:

> ISAIAH 65:17–25. Behold, I will create new heavens and a new earth. The former things will not be remembered, nor will they come to mind. [18] But be glad and rejoice forever in what I will create, for I will create Jerusalem to be a delight and its people a joy. [19] I will rejoice over Jerusalem and take delight in my people; the sound of weeping and of crying will be heard in it no more. [20] "Never again will

there be in it an infant who lives but a few days, or an old man who does not live out his years; he who dies at a hundred will be thought a mere youth; he who fails to reach a hundred will be considered accursed. [21] They will build houses and dwell in them; they will plant vineyards and eat their fruit. [22] No longer will they build houses and others live in them, or plant and others eat. For as the days of a tree, so will be the days of my people; my chosen ones will long enjoy the works of their hands. [23] They will not toil in vain or bear children doomed to misfortune; for they will be a people blessed by the LORD, they and their descendants with them. [24] Before they call I will answer; while they are still speaking I will hear. [25] The wolf and the lamb will feed together, and the lion will eat straw like the ox, but dust will be the serpent's food. They will neither harm nor destroy on all my holy mountain," says the LORD.

The opening sentence of the prophecy deliberately echoes the opening sentence of the Bible: "In the beginning God created the heavens and the earth" (Gen 1:1). What God did in the beginning, says Isaiah, he will do again. The order and perfection of Eden will be restored (and even surpassed).[45]

The verses that follow give us a poetic snapshot of the *physical* dimension of this new creation. Children will all survive and thrive; no-one's young life will be cruelly cut off before it can flourish. This dreaded horror of all parents—a wasted young life—will never take place again. Verse 20 speaks of human longevity: "he who fails to reach a hundred will be considered accursed." This does not mean people die in the new creation. The prophecy is written as a poem (which is why it is set out in stanzas in modern Bibles). Isaiah is engaging in poetic understatement. This is a way of saying that death will no longer have mastery over us in the new creation. This interpretation is confirmed by the earlier reference to the coming kingdom in Isaiah 25:8 where the prophet says that God will "swallow up death for ever". Remember—these are powerful images designed to help us grasp the even greater, hard-to-put-into-words reality of the New Creation.

The physical environment itself, Isaiah goes on, will be prosperous, no longer under a curse: "they will plant vineyards and eat their fruit" (verse 21); "my chosen ones will enjoy the work of their hands" (verse 22); "They will not toil in vain" (verse 23). We must not miss the deliberate echoes here. In Genesis 3 we were told that the physical environment was cursed because of Adam's rejection of the Creator: "Cursed is the ground because of you; through painful toil you will eat of it all the days of your life" (Gen 3:17). Isaiah tells us that this 'toil' with creation will one day be resolved—not *removed* by getting rid of creation altogether but *resolved* by granting blessing where there was curse.

The picture of an ideal physical order climaxes in the final verse of this wonderful passage. We are told that the wolf and the lamb will eat side by side, the lion will eat straw and the serpent will truly bite the dust (verse 25). Almost exactly the same ideas appear earlier in Isaiah, and are said to be the climax of the work of the Messiah (Isa 11:1–9).

It is possible the references to animals in Isaiah 65 (and 11:6–9) are poetic figures for the different nations living in harmony with one another. This would fit the context well enough. But it is equally possible, and we would suggest probable, that Isaiah intends this as a poetic, though nonetheless concrete, description of harmony in the physical world. We are not suggesting Isaiah envisages lions anatomically becoming herbivores. But he may be describing harmony in the animal kingdom. Like so much in Isaiah 65 this too has strong links back to the early chapters of Genesis, where in 2:19–20 Adam is presented with "all the beasts of the field and all the birds of the air" so that he might name them. If Isaiah is deliberately reflecting this 'Edenic' harmony in the animal world, the Sunday School question "Will my dog be in Heaven?" may not be as far off the mark as it first sounds! Perhaps 'my' dog will not get to see the Kingdom but there is good reason to think that animals will be part of God's new creation.

Isaiah foresees a time when all of the ideals of Eden will be restored: when people will be in harmony with each other, when humankind will celebrate its God, when creation will prosper unhindered and when evil will be completely undone. Did you notice the evocative words of verse 25, "dust will be the serpent's food"? This, of course, is a deliberate backward glance to the figure of the serpent in Genesis 3:14 of whom it was said "you will eat dust". The contradictions are resolved, says Isaiah; creation is renewed. That is what the coming kingdom is all about.

13 | Why heaven is not enough

S O WE'VE LOOKED AT THE Old Testament vision of how the contradictions of our world are to be resolved. Is it the same in the New Testament? Is the Christian vision of the Kingdom Come the same as that of biblical Judaism?

Put another way, do the opening chapters of Genesis play the pivotal role in the New Testament vision of the world-to-come that they obviously do in the Old Testament (Isa 65)? Any attentive reader of the (whole) Bible will instinctively say yes, but at least three passages—from three different apostles—confirm this intuition with great clarity.

It is no accident that the final two chapters of the Bible (Rev 21–22) contain more references to the first two chapters of the Bible (Gen 1–2) than do any other part of Scripture. Here is Revelation's vision of the end (perhaps we should say the beginning):

> REVELATION 21:1–5. Then I saw a new heaven and a new earth, for the first heaven and the first earth had passed away, and there was no longer any sea. [2] I saw the Holy City, the new Jerusalem, coming down out of heaven from God, prepared as a bride beautifully dressed for her husband. [3] And I heard a loud voice from the throne saying, "Now the dwelling of God is with men, and he will live with them. They will be his people, and God himself will be

with them and be their God. [4] He will wipe every tear from their eyes. There will be no more death or mourning or crying or pain, for the old order of things has passed away." [5] He who was seated on the throne said, "I am making everything new!" Then he said, "Write this down, for these words are trustworthy and true."

It is obvious that this depiction of the Kingdom Come deliberately draws on Genesis 1 via Isaiah 65. We are told of a new heaven and earth, a new Jerusalem and, in a virtual quotation of Isaiah 65:19, the end of 'death, mourning, crying and pain'.

Rethinking our ideas of heaven

For many of us, even for some long-term Christians, our picture of the Kingdom Come derives from an unlikely collaboration between ancient Greek philosophy and modern movies. The ancient Greek philosopher Plato taught that the physical world is a kind of grubby reflection of the ultimate non-physical reality to which everything is headed. Buddhism and Hinduism share a similar outlook. 'Nirvana' in Buddhism involves the complete cessation of all matter and sensation (as well as consciousness as we usually define it). Hinduism's 'Moksha' is precisely the escape of the *atman* (soul) from the burden of being reborn into the physical world. Hollywood has its own version, almost always portraying the afterlife as an airy-fairy, fourth-dimensional existence with clouds, halos, bright lights and the ever-present harp music. It's otherworldly; it's also a bit creepy!

The Bible says no such things. The Kingdom Come is not an ethereal place of clouds and ghosts but a real place of tangible existence. The physical universe is not a poor dress rehearsal for some naked mental reality called Heaven; this creation is rather a true foretaste, foresight, fore-touch, fore-sound and fore-smell of the new creation God has promised.

But where have we got our ideas of heaven from if not the Bible? Isn't the Bible full of singing angels and white robes and bright lights shining all day long?

The first point to make is that many of the images in the Bible such as these, are describing visions of where God dwells now, not the future Kingdom after resurrection and judgment. When the writer of Revelation has his vision, he is gazing into the throne-room of heaven. And what he describes for us is what he sees God, the Lamb and the angels doing *now*, not in the New Creation. True, the vision is also of "what must soon take place" (Rev 1:1 and 19), but the things that take place do so in the time of judgment, not in the age of eternity when all judgment ceases.

In the age to come, heaven journeys down to earth, God comes to dwell with human beings, and the key image for understanding this is a great city. It is a grand and royal city, described in terms of bedazzling beauty and awesome size, but it is also open to the nations of the earth, whose kings bring in their own splendour (Rev 21:24). In short, it is a heaven-sent place in which the things of earth can dwell.

The biblical images of singing choirs of angels and multitudes in glowing white robes are not depictions of how we will spend eternity. (This is a great relief to those of us who aren't so keen on standing around wearing white.)

Furthermore, elaborate efforts have been made by some theologians and creative thinkers to give heaven a specific structure. It has always been connected with the sky in ancient Greek and Hebrew thought ('the heavens'). Those great ancient thinkers, Pythagoras and Plato, thought that the levels of heaven would be perfectly arranged like harmonics in a musical scale. The medieval writer, Dante, gave heaven ten levels that encompassed the stars and the planets and provided a complicated structure of reward for believers in eternity (more about this in Chapter 14). Dante's heavenly structure had a huge impact on artists for around 600 years. It became popular to draw maps of paradise, with the layers all labelled. Other significant artists—John Milton in his poem *Paradise Lost*, the sixteenth century painter, Sandro Botticelli, and the surrealist Salvador Dali—all produced images of heaven based on Dante's imaginings.

But that is precisely what they are—imaginative, freewheeling expressions of concepts such as perfection, eternity, communion and completion. They are human efforts to get at divine reality, and they move a long way past what we are given in Scripture!

The second point is one we have been making over and over again. We mustn't rush to think that the great imaginative depictions of God's heaven are easily translated into concrete descriptions of what the future creation will be like. We have to let the imagery do its work, and spark in us ideas, concepts, feelings and hopes about what the New Creation will be like, rather than expecting snapshots from the future to carry in our mental pockets until we get there. Our repetition of this idea might be getting boring by now, but it is amazing how reluctant we are to let images be images and not think of them as exactly the way things will be.

Some of the most common examples of images being turned into 'facts' about what eternal life will be like are:

▷ Everyone will have wings like angels. This comes from Matthew 22:30, mingled with descriptions of cherubim from Old Testament books such as 1 Kings and Ezekiel.

▷ People will be playing harps. Again, this idea is a literal reading of Revelation 14:2.

▷ St Peter will be the 'bouncer' at the Pearly Gates. Although most people see this image in cartoons first up, it does have its roots in Revelation 21:21. But there is no mention of Peter there; the idea of Peter in heaven is drawn from Matthew 16:19 where Jesus gives him authority. But this is a very literal jamming together of two Bible passages and is exactly what we must avoid doing.

The Bible offers a wide range of activities and images that help us understand the new creation. We have already mentioned many of them, but others include a marriage feast, resting and feeling safe, rejoicing (as C S Lewis said, "Joy is the serious business of heaven"), enjoying work rather than toiling, and seeing the face of God. We need all of these thoughts and images, in order to grab hold of the reality that lies before us in all of its richness.

Third and finally, we need to admit that many of our ideas of heaven don't come from the Bible at all. They come from that heady mixture of Hollywood, great paintings and not-so-great television shows. Here are some of the non-biblical images of the future creation that we think are most common, and our guess at where people actually get them from:

▷ In heaven we will be gazing at a bright light in a stupified fashion. This probably comes from Dante's famous thirteenth century poem, *The Divine Comedy*, in which the main characters end up seeing a vision of God, having climbed to the highest level of heaven. Dante's impact over hundreds of years on our images of heaven and hell is huge.

▷ Heaven is a starry place somewhere out in deep space, thanks to the Hubble telescope.

▷ Heaven is a desired state of mind, a bit like a happy drug trip or romantic wish fulfilment. This view of heaven props up the movie, *What Dreams May Come*, starring Robin Williams, who searches for his wife and son in a cherub-rich, dream-like landscape. One reviewer called it "an eighty-million-dollar acid-trip fantasy about the pursuit of love in the afterlife". Nothing biblical is going on here.

▷ Heaven is a bit like a Las Vegas variety show. The Monty Python film, *The Meaning of Life*, hams up this 'concert' feel to heaven, in a scene where a cheesy night club singer with perfect teeth croons "It's Christmas in heaven every day of the year' with a troupe of dancing girls and a white staircase in the background.

Heaven on earth

So much for our images of heaven. In fact, the Bible does not envisage us going eternally to *heaven* at all. The intermediate state might be heavenly and spiritual. As we saw in the previous chapter, the Bible says that those who die in Christ's mercy may rest spiritually in the loving presence of God (in heaven). But, as we also saw, this is a *temporary* measure until all the dead are raised, evil is overthrown and the Creator revives his creation. In other words, we do not go to heaven forever; heaven comes to earth. Notice what Revelation 21:2–3 says:

> REVELATION 21:2–3. I saw the Holy City, the new Jerusalem, *coming down out of heaven from* God, prepared as a bride

beautifully dressed for her husband. [3] And I heard a loud voice from the throne saying, "Now the dwelling of God is with men, and he will live *with* them."

The direction is deliberate. The new city comes down out of 'heaven' (which here just means the 'sky') and lands on a new earth, and it is there *on earth* that God himself will dwell with human beings forever. There we will see him face to face (1 Cor 13:12; Matt 5:8). Of course, the idea of God dwelling on earth with mortals comes straight out of Genesis 2 and its description of the Garden of Eden. In fact, as the vision of Revelation 21–22 unfolds, references to the Garden of Eden—with its rivers and trees—come thick and fast. [46]

It is obvious that this is picture language. Much of the book of Revelation is a vision in the apocalyptic style. The absence of the 'sea' (Rev 21:1), for instance, is probably an apocalyptic way of describing the end of evil, since the sea was strongly associated with dark powers in antiquity and in the book of Revelation, in particular, the 'sea' is the Beast's place of origin (Rev 13:1).

But let us not miss the fact that the picture language of Revelation 21–22 is imagery *not of the removal of creation* but of its renewal. John could easily have slipped into the disembodied view of the afterlife so popular in Greco-Roman society. He does not. Under the inspiration of God's Spirit he remains true to the biblical insistence that the Creator will not abandon his creation; he will revive it.

And if there is any doubt remaining about this, two other passages from the New Testament make the same point: God's ultimate intentions for creation are not removal but renewal.

In Romans 8 the Apostle Paul reminds us that the painful contradictions we experience in the world will be resolved not by mankind leaving creation and going to heaven but by God redeeming the creation itself:

> ROMANS 8:18–24. I consider that our present sufferings are not worth comparing with the glory that will be revealed in us. [19] The creation waits in eager expectation for the sons of God to be revealed. [20] For the creation was subjected to frustration, not by its own choice, but by the will of the one who subjected it, in hope [21] that the creation itself will be liberated from its bondage to decay and brought into the glorious freedom of the children of God [that is, the creation will share in the glory of our resurrection]. [22] We know that the whole creation has been groaning as in the pains of childbirth right up to the present time. [23] Not only so, but we ourselves, who have the firstfruits of the Spirit, groan inwardly as we wait eagerly for our adoption as sons, the redemption of our bodies. [24] For in this hope we were saved.

This is an incredibly important theological statement. It is virtually the opposite of Greco-Roman ideas. It places Christianity in stark contrast with many other religions and philosophies—and movies. Our hope is the liberation *of* creation not liberation from it. As verse 21 declares, "the creation itself will be liberated from its bondage to decay and brought into the glorious freedom of the children of God", that is, the freedom of our resurrection. The all-important doctrine of the 'redemption of the body' has its counterpart in the equally important doctrine of the revival of creation. This new Creation is where our bodily resurrection will be lived out forever. Believing in bodily resurrection entails affirming a new creation. We can't have one without the other.

The Apostle Peter speaks of the same hope:

> 2 PETER 3:11–14. You ought to live holy and godly lives [12] as
> you look forward to the day of God and speed its coming.
> That day will bring about the destruction of the heavens by
> fire, and the elements will melt in the heat. [13] But in keeping
> with his promise we are looking forward to a new heaven
> and a new earth, the home of righteousness. [14] So then, dear
> friends, since you are looking forward to this, make every
> effort to be found spotless, blameless and at peace with him.

The phrase "new heaven and a new earth" deliberately recalls
the promise of Isaiah 65:17 which in turn recalls the opening
line of Genesis. What will emerge from the fiery judgment of
God, says Peter, is not the ruin of creation, but its renewal. It is
unclear whether Peter envisages the complete replacement of
this current earth or simply its 'rising from the ashes'. Paul's way
of speaking ("the creation *itself* will be liberated from its bondage
to decay," Rom 8:21) suggests he thought of the new creation as
this world redeemed. But does Peter teach the same thing?

On the one hand, the 'destruction' language in verse 12
sounds pretty decisive: "That day will bring about the destruction
of the heavens." Nevertheless, similar terminology is used just a
few verses earlier to recall the first 'destruction' of the earth in the
Genesis flood story:

> 2 PETER 3:6–7 … the world of that time was deluged and
> *destroyed*. By the same word the present heavens and earth
> are reserved for fire, being kept for the day of judgment and
> *destruction* of ungodly men.

All would agree that the world 'destroyed' by the flood was *this* earth
not some other planet no longer here. If the coming destruction is
similar in Peter's mind to the destruction of the flood, it follows
that Peter thinks it is *this* heaven and earth that will be condemned

and renewed with the arrival of God's kingdom. What is 'destroyed' then are the corruptions of creation not creation *per se*.

Is the promised new heaven and earth *this* world made new or a different universe entirely? Theologians differ because, as you can see, the Scriptures use a range of images and ideas to explore what will take place. What we can say for sure is that there is a definite parallel, especially in Romans 8, between the new creation and our resurrection body. Just as our resurrection bodies will be both continuous and discontinuous with the bodies we live in now, so God's kingdom will be both continuous and discontinuous with the creation we live in now. What God's children will experience in their resurrection, the creation itself will experience in being made new. We cannot be more specific than that.

Boring or glorious?

Some Christians do not really look forward to the Kingdom Come. In our experience this is partly because the version of the 'kingdom' in their heads is the drab, foreign one involving the destruction of all that we know and love here on earth—the sights, the sounds, the sensations, the friendships, the laughter and so on. Or it's the ghostly, strange one which seems more like a dream than reality and about as inviting as a school assembly. But the Bible makes clear that this is not the right framework within which to think about our eternal home, about heaven-come-to-earth. The Old and New Testaments are clear that God the Creator will not abandon his creation; he will renew it, redeem it, resurrect it. Despite the frailties and frustrations we experience this side of Genesis 3, God will make good on the Ideal of Genesis 1 and 2. The picture painted there at the beginning, and reiterated in Isaiah and in the last two chapters of the Bible, provides the true *form and colour* of our future hope.

What we look forward to in the Kingdom is the complete redemption of the spiritual, social and physical dimensions of existence. Just as within history God breathed new life into the lifeless body of Christ, so at the end of history he will once again breathe his life-giving Spirit into the whole cosmos. That is what the Kingdom come *is*. That is something we can all get excited about, for it is a place of tangible beauty and order, a place of life in the fullest sense of the word, a place where the moral and physical contradictions of our current world find resolution through an extraordinary act of divine re-creation.

Living as a new creation

And, finally, as we have so often noted about the Bible's descriptions of our future hope, this coming reality is meant to impinge on the here and now. In the passage quoted above, Peter introduces his teaching about the new creation by saying, "You ought to live holy and godly lives as you look forward to the day of God and speed its coming" (2 Pet 3:11–12). Peter does not mean 'be good' or you might not make it into heaven. Unfortunately, this is often the only link people make between the future and the present, between eschatology and ethics. The Bible does contain some warnings like that but this is not the default connection between hope and godliness.

The biblical connection between eschatology and Christian living goes more like this: since God's kingdom will usher in a world of peace, justice, love, purity and so on, make sure you live by these values already. Practise the kingdom, pre-empt the kingdom, be a sign of the kingdom because, ultimately, the kingdom is the only true and lasting reality. Paul, as we have seen, speaks about living decently and lovingly in this dark world because we can see the first rays of the dawning new day (Rom 13:11–14). Peter puts the same idea in different terms:

> 2 PETER 3:13–14. [W]e are looking forward to a new heaven and a new earth, the home of righteousness. So then, dear friends, since you are looking forward to this, make every effort to be found spotless, blameless and at peace with him.

In other words, since God's kingdom will be the 'home of righteousness', live like you are home already. Put another way, since we are looking forward to a new creation, live as a new creation *now*. Indeed, because God's Spirit dwells in us— guaranteeing the full life of the Spirit in the Kingdom—there is a very real sense in which we already are new creations. As Paul says, "Therefore, if anyone is in Christ, he is a new creation; the old has gone, the new has come!" (2 Cor 5:17). Christians are themselves signs and foretastes of the coming new creation. By God's grace we experience in our lives the death of the 'old' and the resurrection of the 'new'. This is not just a metaphor for trying to live by a new set of rules. By God's Spirit we have already encountered the power of the future—the life breath of the new creation—and he is at work in our mortal bodies calling us to live *now* in anticipation of the Kingdom Come, the 'home of righteousness'.

14 | The Bible's last word

Three dimensions of Christian life

WE BEGAN OUR BOOK by observing how the New Testament repeatedly insists that the Christian life has three dimensions. Without due regard to all of them our perspective will be distorted—less than truly Christian. The three dimensions, of course, are faith, hope and love. Faith is our grateful trust in God's mercy revealed in Jesus' atoning death and resurrection. Love is the chief ethical obligation of all who have faith: we are to love others as the Lord loves us. Then there is hope, the sometimes forgotten dimension of Christian existence. Hope, in biblical-speak, is not a pious wishful thinking; it is rather our eager expectation of the future God has promised in the Bible and previewed in the life, death and resurrection of Jesus.

These three dimensions remind us that as Christians we live for the past, the present and the future. Faith looks back to the cross of Jesus, trusting the mercy and forgiveness of sins he secured there. Love looks squarely at our contemporaries and tries to serve them in Christ's name. And hope looks forward, rejoicing in the knowledge that what we see with the natural eye is not all there is; the eye of hope sees that God has wonderful things in store for us. Faith gives us certainty about these things we hope for, as Hebrews 11:1 tells us, "Now faith is being sure of what we hope for and certain of what we do not see."

We cannot stress enough the importance of this three-dimensional perspective on Christianity. In fact, we suspect many of the problems we encounter in our Christian lives are caused by neglect of one or other of these three dimensions. Neglect *faith* in God's mercy and we will find ourselves burdened with guilt and fearful of the future. Neglect *love* and we will become irrelevant to the world and unrecognisable as followers of Jesus. Neglect *hope* and our life-perspective will shrink, our endurance will wane and our joy will fade.

Some Christian traditions tend to be good at faith and love but don't know what to do with the dimension of hope. They understand the work of Christ on the cross; they champion true charity for our neighbours; but they are timid and quiet about the coming Kingdom. Our book was intended to redress that, urging us all—including ourselves as authors—to turn to God's word and embrace his promises about the future.

The four great promises

There are, we have argued, four essential biblical promises about the future, and we have tried to give each of them their proper place in the various chapters of this book.

The first promise concerns Jesus' return in glory. The Scriptures are clear that the Lord who walked the earth in the first century will come again at the end of history to establish God's kingdom forever. From the perspective of the New Testament this so called 'Second Coming' is the true coming of the Messiah. What occurred in Palestine between 5BC—AD30 was the *preview* not the main feature. The ministry of Jesus recorded in the Gospels has given us advance notice of who the coming Messiah is and what he really stands for. But it is only when he arrives to universal acclaim that the Messiah's mission as foretold in the Old Testament will be properly realised.

The second of the Bible's great promises about the future is also previewed in the ministry of Jesus and fulfilled at the end of time. God has promised to conquer death. Christ's resurrection within history was the pledge and guarantee that all who are *in Christ* will likewise experience what the Apostles' Creed calls "the resurrection of the body and the life everlasting". Eternal life in the Bible, in other words, is not some sort of weird ghostly state. Eternal life is raised, glorified bodily life. God the Creator will not abandon physicality; he will redeem it.

This introduces the Bible's third great promise about the future. The all-important doctrine of the resurrection of the body has its biblical counterpart in the equally important doctrine of the renewal of creation. When the Bible writers dare to describe God's coming Kingdom they don't reach for the imagery of spirits, harps and halos; instead, they take hold of Genesis 1 and 2 and say 'new creation'. According to the repeated teaching of the Bible, God's ultimate intention for creation is not its removal, as in traditional Greek and Hindu thought, but its restoration. The Creator will be faithful to his creation.

The fourth and final promise is, in biblical logic, intimately connected with the restoration of the cosmos. God the Creator will one day overthrow all that is contrary to his wise and just purposes for creation. The theme of Judgment is central to the Bible's vision of the future. As much as contemporary society dislikes it, and as much as the church occasionally misuses the theme, there is no avoiding the fact that the Old and New Testaments say God will right the wrongs of history. Idolaters will be removed, hypocrites will be exposed and all who oppress the weak and needy will find themselves undone by the Lord of justice. He will punish those who don't know God and don't obey the gospel of the Lord Jesus (2 Thess 1:8). In short, those who have not loved God with all their heart and loved their neighbours as themselves will, for this reason, find themselves excluded from God's kingdom and banished to a reality so dire that only the metaphor of *Gehenna*, with its images of darkness, ruin, fire and weeping, is apt to convey its horror.

But God's judgment of the deserving will not be in a blind and arbitrary act of rage. It will be measured, proportional and just—commensurate with a person's deeds. Exactly how people's experience of *Gehenna* will differ, we have no idea. But Jesus insisted that some of the condemned will, in the language of the parable, receive "many blows" and others only a "few" (Luke 12:47–48). Whatever puzzles this idea creates for us, there is comfort in the thought that at the Judgment victims and perpetrators will receive no more and no less than is their due.

Throughout our account of these four great promises about the future we have repeatedly pointed out that God's word sees an intimate connection between the Kingdom Come and life here and now. Eschatology and ethics are intertwined. It is not simply that God's judgment warns us to live in a way that pleases him. The threads run much deeper and are more beautifully woven than that. Christian behaviour is a signpost of the coming rule of God. It truly pre-empts the things that are eternal. There will come a day when injustice will be overthrown and peace will reign, and so we anticipate that future by living justly and in godly unity. There will come a day when human society will be marked by love, and so we look forward to that day by acting with compassion in all things. There will come a day when the knowledge of God will fill the earth, and so we promote the gospel in whatever way we can. We can see the first rays of sunlight of the dawning New Day, and so in eager expectation we live as citizens of the Day even while those around us seem blinded by the night. The new heaven and earth will be the "home of righteousness", as Peter says (2 Pet 3:13). Let us live as if we are already home.

A remaining question

There is a question that arises from all of this. It is one both of us have been asked many times over the years, and in some ways we should have addressed it earlier in the book when we discussed God's judgment. However, we hope you will agree there is value and logic in leaving it until now. The question is: will Christians in any sense be judged according to their deeds? We have said repeatedly throughout the book that those who are shielded by Christ's death will be utterly saved from the judgment of *Gehenna*. But, within this larger truth of a believer's protection from Hell, will the Day of Judgment bring any loss or shame to some Christians and any praise and honour to others? The Bible says 'yes' and 'yes'. Let us explain.

The Apostle Paul writes to the Roman Christians:

ROMANS 14:10–12. ... Why do you look down on your brother? For we will all stand before God's judgment seat. [11] It is written: " 'As surely as I live,' says the Lord, 'every knee will bow before me; every tongue will confess to God.'" [12] So then, each of us will give an account of himself to God.

And to the Corinthians Paul declares:

> 2 CORINTHIANS 5:10. For we must all appear before the judgment seat of Christ, that each one may receive what is due him for the things done while in the body, whether good or bad.

According to these texts, even Christians—who are shielded from condemnation by Christ's death—are not exempt from appearing before the judgment seat of God and Christ. We will not be spectators at the judgment, in other words; we will be called upon to explain why we lived the way we did. That is what it means to "give an account" (Rom 14:12). Moreover, Paul insists that we will receive 'dues' for the good and bad we have done (2 Cor 5:10).

What does this mean for the Christian?

Christians suffering loss

Negatively, this means that the sinful activity of Christians will be exposed as worthless, shameful and deserving of judgment. This is exactly what Paul says of a fellow church worker who, although saved on Judgment Day, will have his shoddy work revealed:

> 1 CORINTHIANS 3:12–15. If any man builds on this foundation using gold, silver, costly stones, wood, hay or straw, [13] his work will be shown for what it is, because the Day will bring it to light. It will be revealed with fire, and the fire will test the quality of each man's work. [14] If what he has built survives, he will receive his reward. [15] If it is burned up, he will suffer loss; he himself will be saved, but only as one escaping through the flames.

Christians will not experience God's wrath itself—shielded as they are by Christ's death—but some, more than others, will feel the 'reverberations' of the judgment that should have been theirs. A good bomb shelter protects you from the blast itself but you still hear the explosion and feel the shock waves. On the Day of Judgment we will know with disturbing clarity which of our actions were worthless and what degree of judgment we have just escaped. The experience will not be lasting—how could it in a perfect new creation!—but it will be serious. There really will be a time of reckoning.

How we behave as followers of Christ really matters. We need not live in fear of Judgment Day but we must live in the knowledge that on that day the Lord will ask each one of us to account for the life we have lived.

Christians receiving honour

What about the positive side of the ledger? Two of the passages quoted above (2 Cor 5:10 and 1 Cor 3:14) suggest that God also intends to reward believers for *good* work. In this, Paul is just following the teaching of Jesus. In the parable of the talents (Matt 25:14–30) and the Parable of the Ten Minas (Luke 19:11–27) servants are given large sums of money: a mina is about 570g (of silver); a talent is 60 minas. The servants are asked to put the money to work for the master. When the accounts are eventually drawn up—a metaphor for Judgment Day—each servant is rewarded according to his faithfulness. As the parable of Luke 19 says:

> LUKE 19:16–19. The first one came and said, 'Sir, your mina [equivalent of 100 days wages] has earned ten more.' [17] "'Well done, my good servant!' his master replied. 'Because you have been trustworthy in a very small matter, take charge of ten cities.' [18] The second came and said, 'Sir, your mina has earned five more.' [19] "His master answered, 'You take charge of five cities.'"

We must not take this parable (and the language of 'reward' generally) and run away into all sorts of speculation. Like so much in the Bible's teaching about judgment, what we have here is picture language. Jesus obviously did not want us to know what his rewards for faithfulness will be—otherwise, he would have told us. He just wants to reassure the faithful that he sees their efforts to bring him honour and he will one day bestow on them honour in return.

It is interesting how often the theme of 'honour' or 'praise' features in descriptions of future rewards (Rom 2:7–10, 29; 1 Cor 4:5; 1 Pet 1:7; 2:7[47]). The same idea is present in the frequent references to races won (1 Cor 9:24), fights carried out (2 Tim 4:7) and 'crowns' bestowed by God on his people on the last day (e.g. 1 Thess 2:19; 2 Tim 2:5; 4:8). The headgear referred to here is not the materially precious crown of a monarch but the simple leaf 'wreath' of the ancient sporting arena, the single purpose of which was to *honour* the winners. As Paul writes: "Everyone who competes in the games goes into strict training. They do it to get a crown that will not last; but we do it to get a crown that will last for ever" (1 Cor 9:25).

And this, we believe, is the best way to think about rewards in God's Kingdom. God intends to publicly *honour* the heroes of faith: the Christian nurse who spent her life serving the destitute in Africa; the persecuted evangelist who preached throughout his beloved China until he was thrown in prison for 20 years; the devout businessman who sacrificed the luxuries of his day so he could give away more than he probably should have; the elderly widow who determined to spend her most useful hours praying for the church and for the world. Of course, such people are not any more 'saved' than the rest of us—and they are probably the last people to expect any honours from the Lord. And please note that, although many of our deeds are obvious, both good and evil, there is no way of *foreknowing* who exactly will receive honours or suffer loss (see 1 Tim 5:24–25). We can simply be certain that either will be deserved, as the veils are drawn back on our lives and all is revealed.

But there is something beautiful about the promise that the Lord will 'praise' our faithfulness. As Paul says of the Judgment Day: "At that time each will receive his praise from God" (1 Cor 4:5). And when it happens there will not be any jealousy or comparison, on our part; there will just be rejoicing that finally faithfulness is lifted up in all its beauty.

John caught a glimpse of such public honour at a wedding reception recently. In speech after speech the parents of the bride, who are former missionaries and tireless servants of Christ and his people, were eloquently praised by the wedding party and relatives for their lifelong compassion, integrity and faith. We have all been to weddings and heard a lot of speeches, but this was different. As each speaker thanked and praised these parents the whole room was nodding and 'mmm'-ing in agreement. There might even have been an 'Amen' or two said under the breath. Some very special people were rightly honoured that day and there was something beautiful—and not at all comparative—about it.

There will come a day when the Lord himself will look the heroes of the faith in the eye and, in the presence of all, declare: "Well done, my good servant! Because you have been trustworthy in a very small matter, take charge of ten cities" (Luke 19:17). And the rest of us will shout "Amen!"

Grace over all

But 'good works' and 'divine rewards' are *not* the place to end a book about God's promised future. One biblical theme stands above Christian faithfulness—above all our faith, hope and love. Under-girding everything in the Christian life and in the Kingdom Come is God's prior *grace*: his free gift of mercy in the death and rising of Jesus.

For all its ominous talk of the judgment to come, Revelation, from which we have drawn so much in our book, has some beautiful ways of reassuring us that God's capacity for grace far exceeds our capacity for faith, hope and love. Perhaps we should repeat that: God's capacity for grace far exceeds our capacity for faith, hope and love.

At the centre of Revelation's final judgment scene is a reminder that salvation is secured not by deeds but by grace. In full apocalyptic style Revelation 20 declares:

> REVELATION 20:12–15. And I saw the dead, great and small, standing before the throne, and books were opened. Another book was opened, which is the book of life. The dead were judged according to what they had done as recorded in the books. [13] The sea gave up the dead that were in it, and death and Hades gave up the dead that were in them, and each person was judged according to what he had done. [14] Then death and Hades were thrown into the lake of fire. The lake of fire is the second death. [15] If anyone's name was not found written in the book of life, he was thrown into the lake of fire.

Critical to the correct interpretation of this vision is the observation that verse 12 introduces two different types of books. First, there is the unnamed set of books said to record the 'works' of every man and woman. You could call these the 'record books' and, of course, we *all* appear in them. Here, then, we meet again the theme of God's proportional judgment: "each person was judged according to what he had done as recorded in the books" (verse 13). For those outside of Christ this will mean condemnation commensurate with their deeds. For those *in* Christ this will mean giving an account of the life we have lived and receiving the honour (and, for some, loss) due to us.

But then there is the separate, single book of verse 12: "Another book was opened, which is the book of life." Notice that it is *this* book, not the record books, which determines our fate. No-one escapes the 'lake of fire' (*Gehenna*) on the basis of what is detailed in the record books: we do not read, "and those who fared well in the books were spared from the lake of fire". Verse 15 is quite clear: it is the second, single volume that holds the key to our destiny: "If anyone's name was not found written in the book of life, he was thrown into the lake of fire." Salvation is all about having one's name written in "the book of life".

The book of life is not a record book like the others. It is not said to contain details of human activity at all. It simply contains names. It is a roll. And if we ask, *What is the criterion for getting my name written in the book of life?*, the book of Revelation has a clear answer. It is entirely to do with Christ's sacrificial death on our behalf. The next reference to this mysterious 'book of life' makes that plain. In Revelation 21:27 we read about who does and does not get into God's Kingdom:

> REVELATION 21:27. Nothing impure will ever enter it, nor will anyone who does what is shameful or deceitful, but only those whose names are written in the *Lamb's* book of life.

In the symbolism of the New Testament, and especially of Revelation, the 'lamb' is always a reference to Jesus as the one, perfect sacrifice for sins, just like the lambs of the Old Testament (who had to be flawless).[48] By calling the Book of Life the *Lamb's* Book of Life (Rev 21:27) Revelation makes clear that the criterion for eternal life is not the record of our deeds but Christ's death (following his flawless life) on our behalf. Jesus died to take our punishment so that, despite the failures written in the record books, the names Greg Clarke and John Dickson could still appear in the Lamb's book of life. Grace, in other words, triumphs over our failures.

John once met a young man years ago at a school near Port Macquarie. For months this 15-year-old had been trying to work out whether or not he was acceptable to God. Without any church contacts he resorted to a kind of personal moral scorecard. He produced an exercise book in which he had drawn what looked like simple accounting columns. Across the top he had written the days of the week and down the left hand column he had listed the virtues he thought the Almighty might be pleased with—'patience', 'kindness' and so on. Then, for each day of the week he had given himself a score out of ten for each virtue. He had pages and pages of records. It was an incredible account of moral struggle—success and failure, over and over again.

Here was the perfect opportunity to share what the Bible says about these things. 'Record books' find us all guilty—his own scoring proved the point—but God offers his mercy freely because of Jesus' death and resurrection. As he listened to this message his face shone and his eyes welled up with tears. He walked over to a bin and with obvious delight threw the record book away. He had realised that grace triumphs over our failures.

As the book of Revelation draws to a close this theme of the triumph of grace is repeated at least twice more.

In Revelation 22:17 we are invited to drink of the grace of God:

REVELATION 22:17. The Spirit and the bride [that is, the church] say, "Come!" And let him who hears say, "Come!" Whoever is thirsty, let him come; and whoever wishes, let him take the free gift of the water of life.

Please soak up the expression, *the free gift of the water of life*. There is nothing complex in this—nothing subtle in the Greek, no historical background needed in order to understand it (although it does allude nicely back to Isaiah 55!). If you want the life God has promised in Jesus Christ, it is yours *freely*—by grace.

And just in case we missed the point, the same pledge of grace reappears in the closing line of Revelation—the closing line of the entire Bible. In a sense, the formal teaching of the book of Revelation climaxes in verse 20 with a statement of hope for Jesus' return:

REVELATION 22:20. He who testifies to these things says, "Yes, I am coming soon." Amen. Come, Lord Jesus.

However, the book has one more thing to say to its readers, to us. Revelation ends—the Bible ends—not with this statement of hope but with a small postscript in verse 21, a parting blessing from the author:

REVELATION 22:21. The grace of the Lord Jesus be with God's people. Amen.

After everything Revelation has told us about the return of Jesus, the overthrow of evil, the resurrection of the dead and the renewal of creation, the book ends not with an exhortation to hope—nor to faith nor love—but with an assurance of God's grace in Christ: the theme above all themes.

Throughout this book the challenge has been to lift our gaze above the tiny horizon of human history we call home and to look forward to the future God has promised in his word. We have been urging us all to be people of increasing hope (as well as increasing faith and love). But even more than this, we long for readers to revel in the knowledge that the '*grace* of the Lord Jesus is with God's people'. For this theme stands above all others.

The free gift of mercy through Jesus Christ surpasses our capacity for faithfulness, covers the multitude of our failings and guarantees us everything God has promised. That is why the Bible's final word is 'grace'. That is why our final word is grace.

Endnotes

1. Lahaye, T. and Jenkins, J., *Left Behind* Series, Tyndale House.
2. He can't finish the letter without repeating the same idea: 1 Thessalonians 5:8–9. Let us be self-controlled, putting on *faith* and *love* as a breastplate, and the *hope* of salvation as a helmet.
3. In fact, we stopped at this point and did exactly that: we picked a page at random (just once) and read the words, "Speak and act as those who are going to be judged by the law that gives freedom, because judgment without mercy will be shown to anyone who has not been merciful. Mercy triumphs over judgment!" (Jas 2:12–13). And just four verses earlier (verse 8) James quotes Leviticus 19:18 as saying "Love your neighbour as yourself." Future hope and present love right next to each other.
4. Some of us are used to thinking of Jesus' death as occurring in AD 33, not AD 30. Either is possible but most New Testament historians go with the earlier date. For convenience, we follow the majority.
5. This is not to deny that in another sense believers already possess 'eternal life' (E.g. John 4:24; 6:54).
6. Or as the prophet Joel puts it:
   Joel 2:28–32. "And afterwards, I will pour out my Spirit on all people. Your sons and daughters will prophesy, your old men will dream dreams, your young men will see visions. Even on my servants, both men and women, I will pour out my Spirit in those days. I will show wonders in the heavens and on the earth, blood and fire and billows of smoke. The sun will be turned to darkness and the moon to blood before the coming of the great and dreadful day of the LORD. And everyone who calls on the name of the LORD will be saved; for on Mount Zion and in Jerusalem there will be deliverance, as the LORD has said, among the survivors whom the LORD calls."

   Interestingly, in the book of Acts the Apostle Peter sees this prophecy of Joel as partially fulfilled on the day of Pentecost when the gathered believers received the Holy Spirit and spoke in the languages of the nations around about. Peter says: "These men are not drunk, as you suppose. It's only nine in the morning! No, this is what was spoken by the prophet Joel" (Acts 2:15–16). Peter cannot mean that everything in the Joel passage has been fulfilled;

obviously, the 'great and dreadful day of the Lord' is yet to come. He means that the ultimate outpouring of God's Spirit associated with the final kingdom has begun in the gift of the Spirit given on the day of Pentecost (and whenever someone turns to Christ). The future has come into the present.

7. The same reality is described in Romans 8:23–24 using the metaphor of the initial 'fruits' of the coming harvest: "Not only so, but we ourselves, who have the *firstfruits of the Spirit*, groan inwardly as we wait eagerly for our adoption as sons, the redemption of our bodies. For in this hope we were saved."

8. The Apostle Paul tells us how to think properly about sin in the Christian life: we are to strive to overcome it. "Not that I have already obtained this or am already perfect, but I press on to make it my own, because Christ Jesus has made me his own" (Phil 3:12). We are to *strive* to be perfect, as our heavenly Father is, in the same way that you strive to run down the final stretch of a race towards the finish line. The finish line is, of course, still ahead of us.

9. *Sydney Morning Herald*, September 29, 2005.

10. Revelation 17:9 almost gives it away (for dummies): "This calls for a mind with wisdom. The seven heads are seven hills on which the woman sits." Everyone knew Rome was the city founded on seven hills.

11. The sorry tale is fully reported in three *Sydney Morning Herald* articles: "On special: tickets to heaven", *SMH* 01/09/1992; "Apocalypse Now(ish)", *SMH* 01/10/1992; "No sudden vanishings in Gladesville", *SMH* 30/10/1992.

12. Steve Turner, *Up to Date*. London: Hodder and Stoughton, 1983, pp72–73. (Permission sought).

13. Paul Helm, *The Last Things*, Banner of Truth, Edinburgh, 1989, p. 35.

14. Rousseau, quoted in Enright, *The Oxford Book of Death,* (Oxford University Press, Oxford, 1983), p. 22.

15. The famous Christian writer, C. S. Lewis, seems to have held something akin to a belief in purgatory. He thought that Christians needed to be 'cleaned' for heaven, and compared the process to sitting in a dentist's chair before judgment day and then waking up after the treatment to rinse out your mouth! However, it is our view that the 'cleaning' is accomplished through Christ's death as we turn to obey the gospel (and then as God's Spirit continues to work in us throughout our Christian lives). We do not need some post-death, pre-Judgment Day spruce-up. As Peter writes: "Now that you have purified yourselves by obeying the truth so that you have sincere love for your brothers, love one another deeply, from the heart" (1 Pet 1:22).

16. There is one reference in Scripture to a 'second' appearance of Jesus, so the language of a 'Second Coming' is not completely unbiblical: Hebrews 9:28 says, "he will appear a second time, not to bear sin, but to bring salvation to those who are waiting for him." This is the exception that proves the rule.

17. Most commentaries on 1 Thessalonians offer the details, as does the book by eminent New Testament scholar Ben Witherington III, *Jesus, Paul and the End of the World: a Comparative Study in New Testament Eschatology*. IVP, 1992, pp. 152–161.

18. It is possible the parable of the Sheep and the Goats (Matt 25:31–46) refers to the neglect of the *believing* poor, rather than the poor generally. Jesus does describe the hungry and thirsty of the parable as "these *brothers* of mine" which may plausibly refer directly to Christians (or, on another view, Jewish Christians). However, a long line of experts takes a different view (including John Chrysostom, Joachim Jeremias, Charles Cranfield, David Wenham, John P. Meier, William D. Davies and Dale C. Allison). These scholars suggest that 'brothers' here refers to those for whom the coming Messiah, the defender of the needy, feels deep sympathy. 'Brothers' then simply means 'friends' (as in Acts 3:17). More importantly, there is something inherently implausible about the idea that God will judge "all the nations" (v. 32) on the basis of how they treat poor *Christians*. Most men and women around the world have never even seen a needy Christian, let alone had the opportunity to feed and clothe one. How could God judge the *entire world* on this basis? The poor more broadly, on the other hand, have always existed in human societies, providing people with a real litmus test of their compassion and another reason for God to call us to account. Regardless of how we interpret the 'brothers' in Matthew 25:31–46, it would be shameful to suggest that God expects us to care for the Christian poor only. That would contradict what Jesus says in the parable of the Good Samaritan (Luke 10:25–37). Here Jesus demands that practical mercy be shown *across* racial and religious boundaries. In fact, the parable was first told as a rebuke to someone who had tried to justify his restrictive definition of 'neighbour' (Luke 10:29). Our poverty-stricken brothers and sisters in Christ will no doubt be the main recipients of Christian aid—they are our 'family', after all—but it must not stop there. As the Apostle Paul said, "Therefore, as we have opportunity, let us do good to *all* people, *especially* to those who belong to the family of believers" (Gal 6:10).

19. "On special: tickets to heaven," *Sydney Morning Herald,* 01/09/1992.

20. George Orwell, "As I Please", *Tribune*, 14 April 1944. Online at http://orwell.ru/library/articles/As_I_Please/english/eaip_01.Retrieved 1/2/07.

21. We chose the NRSV for our quotation of Luke 20:47 because, strangely, the NIV has "such men will be punished *most* severely." Here they have rendered a Greek comparative (*perissōteros:* 'more', 'greater') with the ambiguous English adjective 'most'. There is no ambiguity in the Greek. The *New Revised Standard Version* translates it perfectly (so also the new *English Standard Version*).

22. Jesus spoke of "the coming wrath" (Matt 3:7), and is in fact an agent of this wrath in Revelation 6, where the "wrath of the Lamb" (a strange image!) is to

be feared: "For the great day of their wrath has come, and who can stand?" (Rev 6:17).

23. Perhaps Jesus might have considered it to begin with the beheading of John the Baptist, and therefore would himself have expected to suffer on the way to deliverance.

24. The Preterist view considers the Temple's destruction to be a judgment in the here-and-now on the Jews who rejected Christ as Messiah. The broader Historicist view is that God uses various figures in history (various 'antichrists', you might say) to judge Jews for their disobedience to the Messiah. Needless to say, this view often brings on the charge of anti-Semitism!

25. John remembers a pastor friend saying he believed Mother Theresa was the Antichrist—and he was serious! The logic (if that's the right word) was that Mother Theresa gave such a good impression of Roman Catholicism to the world, she must have been of the devil.

26. The point is reiterated in Deuteronomy 24:14–15, "Do not take advantage of a hired man who is poor and needy, whether he is a brother Israelite or an alien living in one of your towns. Pay him his wages each day before sunset, because he is poor and is counting on it. Otherwise he may cry to the LORD against you, and you will be guilty of sin."

27. It is true that the terms 'poor' and 'needy' are sometimes used in Isaiah and elsewhere to refer to humble, faithful Israelites. However, the description of the Messiah's defence of the poor in Isaiah 11:1–4 follows hot on the heels of the prophet's denunciation of Israel's mistreatment of the economically poor: "Ah, you who make iniquitous decrees, who write oppressive statutes, to turn aside the needy from justice and to rob the poor of my people of their right, that widows may be your spoil, and that you may make the orphans your prey!" (Isa 10:1–4).

28. As the writer to the Hebrews affirms: "it is impossible for the blood of bulls and goats to take away sins" (Heb 10:5).

29. A distinction is usually made in theology between general revelation and special revelation. General revelation refers to what is revealed about God through creation itself. Special revelation refers to what is revealed about God through his explicit word (whether in the Torah or the gospel). The distinction is an important one but it would be a mistake to believe, as is sometimes thought, that general revelation only condemns us and special revelation only saves us. It is truer to say that without the work of God's Spirit in our hearts both types of revelation condemn us; and *with* the work of God's Spirit in our hearts both types of revelation illuminate true faith. So, the true believer (in whom God's Spirit is working) looks at creation and is able to 'hear' God's silent word about himself (Psa 19:1–6). To this person, general revelation functions like special

revelation (one in which God speaks). The unbeliever, however, hears the gospel word and refuses to repent. For this person, the special revelation in the gospel is as 'dumb' as the general revelation in creation.

30. It might be thought that if God showed mercy to someone without knowledge of the gospel it would contradict the principle that true faith arises only from God's word (Rom 10:17). But this assumes that God cannot speak through creation itself. Psalm 19:1–6 insists that the heavens do indeed declare the glory of God. As we said in the previous note, the unbeliever is completely deaf to this 'word' (so says Paul in Rom 1:18–25). But the person in whom God's Spirit is at work hears this word and, like the psalmist, offers praise to the God of creation.

31. Numbers 18:21

32. The discussion of Melchizedek in Hebrews 7 confirms the interpretation that this figure was righteous in God's eyes.

33. More interesting is the connection with Psalm 141:2 where a faithful Israelite asks that his prayers be counted as a temple sacrifice pleasing to the Lord: "May my prayer be set before you like incense; may the lifting up of my hands be like the evening sacrifice."

34. It might be argued that the divine 'acceptance' Peter mentions in Acts 10:34–35 is a reference to Cornelius' acceptance of the gospel *at the end of the chapter* not a reference to Cornelius' prayers and charity described earlier in the chapter. This is difficult to sustain. Notice that Luke introduced us to Cornelius back in verse 2 by emphasizing exactly two things about him: he feared God (as indicated by his regular prayers) and he was good to others (as indicated by his gifts to the poor). In other words, he obeyed the universal twofold obligation. The angel reiterates the point just two verses later saying to Cornelius, "Your prayers and gifts to the poor have come up as a memorial offering before God" (10:4). And, just in case we missed the pattern, verse 22 restates the same thing: "He is a righteous and God-fearing man." In light of this repeated twofold description of Cornelius as a man who reveres God and cares for people, Peter's words in verses 34–35 contain an unmistakable reference to Cornelius' status as a man acceptable to God: "I now realise how true it is," says Peter, "that God does not show favouritism but accepts men from every nation who fear him and do what is right" (10:34–35). The twofold 'fear God' and 'do what is right' must summarize what has been said about Cornelius so far.

The eminent British historian F. F. Bruce has offered a different account insisting that Cornelius was not saved until after his acceptance of Peter's message. His argument is based on Acts 11:14 where, in Peter's retelling of the whole Cornelius episode, the Apostle explains what the angel said to Cornelius in his vision: "He (Peter) will bring you a message through which you and all your household *will be saved.*" Bruce concludes from this that these Gentiles were not in true relationship with God until after they believed the gospel. To us it seems unnatural to allow a passing comment in the middle of Acts 11 to overturn the carefully crafted description of Cornelius throughout chapter 10 as a man of faith and obedience. It is far better to find a way of understanding 11:14 in light of the total portrait offered in 10:1–35. There are a couple of solutions: (1) the expression "will be saved" refers to Cornelius' final salvation on the last day which, obviously, will be based on the gospel now that his faith has its proper content; (2) the reference to the 'message' through which Cornelius would be saved is a shorthand way of saying that Peter's message will explain the *things* upon which Cornelius' salvation are based, i.e., the death and resurrection of Jesus. The plural term *rhēmata* translated here as 'message' often does refer to the *things* contained in a message rather than the message itself (e.g., Luke 2:19, "Mary treasured up all these *things* and pondered them in her heart"). An excellent article critiquing F. F. Bruce and outlining a case similar to our own was written years ago by Glenn N. Davies, "When was Cornelius saved?" *The Reformed Theological Review* Vol.46 (no.2), 1987, 43–49.

35. We should probably repeat something we said earlier. If (hypothetically) Cornelius had rejected the message of Peter, this would be evidence that his prayers and charity were not the expression of true faith but simply a hollow attempt at religion. True faith always responds rightly to the revelation of God.

36. Whatever one's view of the origin of our species, the central claim of the Genesis narrative is a universal one: Adam's story is the story of all humanity (a point underlined by the fact that 'Adam' in Hebrew means Man or Mankind).

37. This is why Jesus' healings by the power of the Holy Spirit are said to be proof that the coming Kingdom of God was already here (Matt 12:28). This is also why Paul can say that the gift of the Holy Spirit now is a "deposit guaranteeing our inheritance" (Eph 1:14). That 'inheritance' is the Spirit-infused world to come, of which the indwelling of the Holy Spirit is a foretaste. These are the ideas which lie behind Paul's deceptively simple phrase 'spiritual body'.

38. This connection between our future resurrection bodies and God's Spirit is stated plainly in Romans 8:11, "And if the Spirit of him who raised Jesus from the dead is living in you, he who raised Christ from the dead will also give life to your mortal bodies through his Spirit, who lives in you."

39. The idea that our resurrection body is modelled on Jesus' resurrection body is also found in Philippians 3:20–21—"But our citizenship is in heaven. And we eagerly await a Saviour from there, the Lord Jesus Christ, who, by the power that enables him to bring everything under his control, will transform our lowly bodies so that they will be like his glorious body."

40. There are just two other New Testament uses of the term 'Paradise'. In 2 Corinthians 12:4 it appears to be a reference to God's current abode, i.e. what we normally think of as 'heaven'. However, in Revelation 2:7 paradise is clearly the new Eden (or creation) wherein the faithful will have the "right to eat from the tree of life".

41. Web reference: http://www.sermonaudio.com/sermoninfo.asp?currSection=sermonsbible&sermonID=3300317514.

42. The only other Old Testament passage to herald this worldwide destruction is found in the brief prophecy of Zephaniah. This book contains a gloomy message of judgment for the rebellious kingdom of Judah, but it is cast in the broader, cosmic apocalyptic framework:

> Zeph 1: 2–3. "I will sweep away everything from the face of the earth," declares the Lord. "I will sweep away both men and animals; I will sweep away the birds of the air and the fish of the sea. The wicked will have only heaps of rubble when I cut off man from the face of the earth."

> Zeph. 1:18. …In the fire of his jealousy the whole world will be consumed, for he will make a sudden end of all who live in the earth.

This book of prophecy emphasises the day of the Lord which is coming with wrath, distress and anguish because of people's sins. Once again, the emphasis is on punishing the sinner with such ferocity that the earth itself suffers.

43. Another theory is that the word *harmagedōn* in Greek is a corruption of a Hebrew description of Jerusalem (*har migdo* = 'mountain of fruitfulness'; *har mo'ed* = 'mountain of assembly'). On this view, the final battle will take place on Zion, Israel's sacred mountain.

44. *The Telegraph* (London), Wednesday May 10, 1995.

45. Of course, the other dimension spoken of in Genesis 2 is the *social* dimension: human beings at one with each another, and Isaiah says this too will be restored in the new creation. That is what the 'new Jerusalem' is all about. The historical city of Jerusalem had once been a centre for social and spiritual celebration. And this is precisely what Isaiah envisages being revived in the 'new Jerusalem'. A new social-spiritual reality will pervade God's eternal kingdom: "for I will create Jerusalem to be a delight and its people a joy" (verse 1).

46. Revelation 22:1–3. Then the angel showed me the river of the water of life, as clear as crystal, flowing from the throne of God and of the Lamb [2] down the middle of the great street of the city. On each side of the river stood the tree of life, bearing twelve crops of fruit, yielding its fruit every month. And the leaves of the tree are for the healing of the nations. [3] No longer will there be any curse.

47. For some reason, many English translations of 1 Peter 2:7 have something like the NIV: "Now to you who believe, this stone is precious." But the great

majority of commentators translate the sentence very differently. The Greek words *humin* (to you) *oun* (therefore) *tē timē* (the honour) *tois pisteuousin* (to those believing) mean something like "The honour is for you who believe".

48. Revelation 5:8–9 has already firmly established the image of Jesus as a 'lamb' as a reference to his perfect sacrifice or sins: '[T]he four living creatures and the twenty-four elders fell down before the *Lamb*. Each one had a harp and they were holding golden bowls full of incense, which are the prayers of the saints. [9]And they sang a new song: "You are worthy to take the scroll and to open its seals, because you were slain, and with your blood you purchased men for God from every tribe and language and people and nation."'